**OFFICE OF THE
DEPUTY PRIME MINISTER**

Equality and Diversity in Local Government in England

A literature review

May 2003
Sarah Morgan, Local and Regional Government Research Unit, ODPM
Office of the Deputy Prime Minister: London

Following the reorganisation of the government in May 2002, the responsibilities of the former Department for Transport, Local Government and the Regions (DTLR) in this area were transferred to the Office of the Deputy Prime Minister.

Office of the Deputy Prime Minister
Eland House
Bressenden Place
London SW1E 5DU
Telephone 020 7944 4400
Web site www.odpm.gov.uk

Further copies of this publication are available from:
Office of the Deputy Prime Minister Publications
PO Box 236
Wetherby LS23 7NB

Tel: 0870 1226 236
Fax: 0870 1226 237
Textphone: 0870 1207 405
Email: odpm@twoten.press.net
or online via the Office of the Deputy Prime Minister's web site.

ISBN 1 85112 621 X

Printed in Great Britain on material containing 75% post-consumer waste and 25% ECF pulp (cover) and 100% post-consumer waste (text).

May 2003

Product Code 03 LG 01192

CONTENTS

4 LOCAL AUTHORITIES AND SERVICES 61

5 CONCLUSIONS 75

BIBLIOGRAPHY 78

ANNEX A

LIST OF TABLES

TABLES IN APPENDICES

EXECUTIVE SUMMARY

This report provides an overview of recent literature, which examines how local authorities in England have dealt with issues of equality and diversity. Three themes are covered in relation to equality and diversity: representation and participation; employment; services. There is a range of literature dealing with ethnic minorities and women and their experiences of local government. The small body of literature dealing with young people's participation in local government is also examined in the review. In contrast, there is little or no literature dealing with sexual orientation, disability, and class in the context of local government. While there is a large body of literature dealing with housing and social services provision, and which is beyond the scope of this overview, there is little which looks at equality in service provision holistically and across the range of local authority activity.

The report is divided into five chapters: chapter 1 is a brief overview of equal opportunities in English local authorities in the 1980s and 1990s; chapter 2 deals with representation and participation in local government; chapter 3 with employment by local authorities; chapter 4 looks at the limited literature on incorporating equality and diversity into service provision by local authorities; chapter 5 offers some brief conclusions.

CHAPTER 1: LOCAL AUTHORITIES AND EQUAL OPPORTUNITIES

By the 1980s, many local authorities had developed equal opportunities policies. The impetus for this arose from new legislation (1975 Sex Discrimination Act; 1976 Race Relations Act), as well as lobbying by community and women's groups. The focus of these policies was often, but not exclusively, on women and ethnic minority groups and particularly their access to employment within local authorities. Programmes of awareness training were also developed by some local authorities for their staff.

By the end of the 1980s, equal opportunities policies in local government had been partly discredited; in particular, equal opportunities were associated by some with 'loony left' councils. However, while the success of equal opportunities policies in local government were questioned, it should be acknowledged that local government was in advance of the private sector in addressing these issues. By the 1990s, the commitment to equality was placed in a different context. The Macpherson Report, 1995 Disability Discrimination Act and the 2000 Race Relations (Amendment Act) all placed new and different pressures or duties on local authorities in terms of delivering equality and diversity.

The Government's commitment to a modernisation agenda for local government includes the promotion of a meaningful equality and diversity agenda. This is based on the assumption that local authorities which are representative and inclusive are better able to deliver satisfactorily to their local communities, and will demonstrate better and more inclusive leadership styles. The White Paper *Strong Local Leadership: Quality Public Services* emphasises the need for democratic accountability, community cohesion and civic renewal. Specific mention is made of the need to recognise that 'Local areas are becoming more diverse' (2001: 13) and the need for councils to hear all voices. New legislation dealing with the Employment Directive and the Race Directive will also impact on the range of local authority activities including employment practices, consultation with communities and, service delivery and procurement.

Little or nothing is said in this literature review regarding other groups which are under-represented in local government and/or to which equality and diversity issues and policies apply. Literature on disabled people and young people is sparse. More specifically, no literature was found relating to the experiences of lesbians, gays, bisexuals and transgender people or about nomadic ethnic groups. Yet local councils have a wide impact on these and other groups. There is, however, a current ESRC-funded research project which aims to examine local council policies on lesbians, gays and bisexuals in the time period 1990–2001[1]. Little is known about the participation of nomadic groups in democratic processes in Britain, although the informed guess must surely be that participation is very low, given the difficulties faced by nomadic groups since the abolition of the duty to supply halting sites and high rates of illiteracy. For nomadic groups, contact with most local authorities is negative and involves being evicted from an unofficial halting site. There is also an absence of comment on the issue of class in terms of local authority representation, participation, employment and services.

CHAPTER 2: REPRESENTATION AND PARTICIPATION

At present, and despite concerns raised in a number of reports, dating back to the Maud Committee in 1967, there has been little change in the socio-economic profile of councillors. Women, ethnic minorities, young people, people in paid employment, and non-professionals are under-represented in the council chamber. Widening the pool of people from which councillors are drawn would appear to be a necessary step in broadening the representativeness of elected members, if actual representation is a desirable outcome. While this review has not specifically examined the role of the political parties in this, it is apparent that, as the main conduit for elected members, they continue to have an important part to play in efforts to enhance the representativeness of elected members in local councils.

Barriers which deter participation as elected representatives are wider than any which may reside in the political parties, and in part reflect modern society and its demands. One of the biggest challenges for local government is to overcome the high levels of disinterest in both local elections and local authority activities generally. It appears that many people feel that the time demands of acting as a local councillor are too onerous, and difficult to fit in with the burdens of work and home. Those who do feel that they have the time to give to local councils as elected members are disproportionately likely to be retired: 37.5 per cent of councillors gave their occupation as retired in the 2001 Local Government Census.

The literature survey found that the experiences of women and ethnic minority councillors were relatively well-documented. There is a small body of literature dealing with young people's experiences of participation in local government. In terms of other under-represented groups, the literature is sparse. Disabled people may find access to the most basic element of the democratic process – voting – difficult when they choose to vote in person, rather than by postal ballot or proxy. Employed people find it difficult to fit in council duties with work and home life. Nothing in the literature surveyed deals with sexual orientation and elected membership.

More women stood down at the last set of local elections than were newly elected as councillors; the proportion of ethnic minority councillors also decreased between 1997 and 2001. The larger body of work available on the experiences of women councillors and councillors from ethnic minority groups indicates that within councils, there are issues of sexism and racism which impact negatively on experiences of being a local councillor and

---

1 Davina Cooper, Jean Carabine and Surya Munro *The Changing Politics of Lesbian and Gay Equality in Local Government, 1990–2001.*

which may contribute to decisions to stand down. Whether the re-organisation of councils (that is, the development of executives and scrutiny panels) has any effect on this remains to be seen.

There is some evidence that women councillors see themselves primarily as community representatives, rather than as politicians. Being a local representative does place demands on the work-life balance, especially for women with family and caring responsibilities. However, this might be seen as preferable to involvement in national politics which, although properly remunerated (thereby eliminating conflict with employment), can mean extended periods of time away from home. This preference means that for some women councillors, council membership may not be viewed as a stepping stone to involvement in national politics.

People from ethnic minorities are under-represented as councillors, although in some urban areas it is believed that there may be over-representation. For councillors from an ethnic minority, an inherent danger is that they will be promoted as proof of inclusion, while simultaneously experiencing exclusionary and even racist behaviour from other councillors and officers. There is some evidence that the selection of ethnic minority candidates has been confined to wards where 'race' is perceived to be a relevant factor, ie wards which have or are believed to have a higher than average proportion of ethnic minority voters. There is very little evidence to suggest that, once elected, ethnic minority councillors have a positive impact on relations between local authorities and ethnic minority populations. Indeed, there is some evidence that ethnic minority voters have low opinions of ethnic minority councillors from the same ethnic group as themselves.

The particular concern regarding young people is that they are disengaged from mainstream politics and do not vote. The disinterest of young people in local government reflects a wider disinterest in society, although this trend may be stronger among young voters. Numbers of young councillors aged under twenty five in England are tiny, underscoring the elderly age profile of councillors in general. There is limited evidence regarding young people's participation in local government; what evidence there is suggests that mechanisms introduced to encourage participation may be consultative rather than inclusive. Additionally, young people who have been involved in these participatory exercises have not always felt that they were really listened to, thus undermining the purpose and intent of these participatory mechanisms.

CHAPTER 3: EMPLOYMENT IN LOCAL AUTHORITIES

Just under three quarters of local authority employees are women. In contrast, ethnic minority employees are, on average, under-represented in local authority workforces relative to their population size in England. There are very few women or ethnic minority chief executives and there is also under-representation at chief officer level. This is despite the gains made from, in some cases, over 20 years of equal opportunity policies in employment.

The literature identifies a 'glass ceiling' through which many women and ethnic minority employees in local government find it difficult to pass through. In addition, problems remain if promotion is secured: the evidence cited here is that senior women and ethnic minority staff do face discrimination, including direct discrimination. This has a negative impact on those who have not broken through the glass ceiling: for women there is evidence that the attitude of male senior staff and elected members towards women senior staff is a factor in deciding against applying for promotion.

The flexible working practices offered by many local authorities, and especially larger authorities, are also attractive to women, who make up the vast majority of local authority employees. Schemes vary from authority to authority, but can include jobshares, flexible hours and school term working, for example. However, both vertical and horizontal segregation is apparent across the different sectors of local authority employment, suggesting that some sectors are more woman-friendly than others. In particular, part-time women manual workers tend to be neglected in the implementation of equal opportunities policies, and flexible working may be something which is imposed rather than chosen.

Both women and ethnic minority managers working in local authorities report that they experience more barriers in climbing the career ladder than do their men and white counterparts. Ethnic minority employees are more likely than white colleagues to have had a diverse career before joining a local authority. White managers report having wider responsibilities and more staff to manage than do their ethnic minority peers.

In terms of recruitment, women and black officers have expressed concern about the role which elected members play in selection of officers, which they believe is to the detriment of women and ethnic minority candidates. In addition, while women and ethnic minority managers do have aspirations to reach the top (chief executive), this is tempered by concerns about becoming isolated as the career ladder is scaled.

CHAPTER 4: LOCAL AUTHORITIES AND SERVICES

Local authorities are an important deliverer of services to the local communities they serve. As a major provider of services, either directly or indirectly through sub-contracting, local government has an important role in the promotion of equality and diversity. Demographic information can be used to identify sub-groups of the population, which may have different or particular service needs compared to the general local population. The replacement of Compulsory Competitive Tendering (CCT) by Best Value enables local authorities to give consideration to wider issues than just cost in service delivery. The development of performance indicators, including those based on user satisfaction surveys, provides local authorities with baseline data on their services. Data from the user satisfaction surveys shows that, overall, ethnic minority users tend to express more dissatisfaction than do white British service users.

Reducing social exclusion implies that services should meet the needs of the most disadvantaged in order to ameliorate or alleviate that disadvantage. But there is scant evidence that local authorities have moved to a position of implementing equality and diversity in order to promote social inclusion. Policies to promote social inclusion have tended to focus on housing and the areas of worst deprivation. This may mean that some areas and some groups, such as owner occupiers in deprived and run-down areas, may miss out from initiatives.

By the 1990s, the shift to consumer oriented services did deliver changes in service delivery, including monitoring of service users in order to ascertain need and quality of service received. A flaw with this approach is that it cannot deliver any information about who does not use a service and why. The business case for diversity emphasises a match between employees and service users: however, this approach to equality and diversity could mean that employees are assumed to be able to deliver appropriate services because of their social characteristics, rather than ability or training.

CHAPTER 5: CONCLUSIONS

It is important not to see the three themes examined in this review (representation, participation and leadership, employment, and service delivery) as separate from each other. Policies, including those on equal opportunities or equality, are developed by officers and approved by elected members. While the three strands do overlap and can be mutually reinforcing, this does not necessarily imply a positive or negative relationship among them.

Local authorities have been trailblazers in the field of equalities and there are many examples of good and best practice to be found in this sector. Local authorities are important sources of employment for women and ethnic minority people, for example. Flexible working policies can be important for employees which have family and/or caring responsibilities. However, good practice in recruitment has not always been followed through to ensure equal opportunities in promotion and development. There is also some evidence that there are some problems of sexism and racism for staff within local authorities, coming from both fellow staff and members. These problems cut across the three themes examined in this literature review.

There is a public sector case to be made for equality and diversity which is analogous to the business case, but different from it. As with the business case, this encompasses issues of fairness in employment practices (recruitment, retention, development and training), having a good reputation, access to a wider client or customer base and the avoidance of expensive litigation as a consequence of discrimination. However, for the public sector, there are also issues of equality of access and representation which are not apparent in the business case.

CHAPTER 1

Local Authorities and Equal Opportunities

1.1 Introduction

This report provides an overview of recent literature, mainly in the last seven years, which deals with how local authorities have dealt with issues of equality and diversity. The barriers which women and people from ethnic minorities face in becoming councillors and as local authority employees are relatively well-documented, as the space given to discussion of these areas attests. Concern about young people's lack of participation in electoral politics tends to focus on the national level. However, there is also a small, and growing, body of literature concerned with young people's participation in local government which is discussed here.

The review offered here is limited in both terms of scope and time. Representation and participation in local politics, and employment in local authorities, for disabled people, and gay, lesbian, bisexual and transgender people is absent from the literature reviewed here. In addition, there is very little literature which examines local authorities efforts to implement policies on equality and diversity in terms of service provision. It is likely that there are reports published by local authorities themselves (for example, community care plans may refer to population characteristics in the local area in order to justify service provision and modes of delivery) and community groups. Reviewing this literature, however, is beyond the scope of this report. In terms of time, the review is again limited as it tends not to include literature from before the mid-1990s. However, much of the literature cited in this report refers back to and reviews earlier literature.

1.1.1 GAPS IN THE REVIEW

Little or nothing is said in this literature review regarding other groups which are under-represented in local government and/or to which equality and diversity issues and policies apply. Literature on disabled people and young people is sparse. More specifically, no literature was found relating to the experiences of lesbians, gays, bisexuals and transgender people or about nomadic ethnic groups. Yet local councils have a wide impact on these and other groups. With respect to lesbians, gays, bisexuals and transgender people, most of the literature regarding local governance is rather old and specifically deals with the Section 28 restrictions on teaching about homosexual lifestyles and sexualities in school sex education classes. There is, however, a current ESRC-funded research project which aims to examine local council policies on lesbians, gays and bisexuals in the time period 1990–2001.[1] Little is known about the participation of nomadic groups in democratic processes in Britain, although the informed guess must surely be that participation is very low, given the difficulties faced by nomadic groups since the abolition of the duty to supply halting sites and high rates of illiteracy. For

---

1 Davina Cooper, Jean Carabine and Surya Munro *The Changing Politics of Lesbian and Gay Equality in Local Government, 1990–2001.*

nomadic groups, contact with most local authorities is negative and involves being evicted from an unofficial halting site.

In particular, there is an absence of comment on the issue of class in terms of local authority representation, participation, employment and services. The profile of councillors is increasingly middle class and professional, suggesting that this is also an area for further exploration. This consolidation towards more professional, middle class councillors may reinforce perceptions that councillors are remote. A class bias also pertains in the literature on employment by local authorities in that it focuses on the professional sector. Yet there are issues of equality and diversity to be addressed in the manual professions.

1.1.2 REPORT STRUCTURE

The report is divided into three main thematic areas: chapter two deals with representation and participation in local government; chapter three with employment by local authorities; finally chapter four looks at the very limited literature on service provision by local authorities, and offers a secondary analysis of the Best Value performance indicator which measures satisfaction with the overall service provided by local authorities (BVPI 3) from the user satisfaction surveys of 2001/2. Firstly, however, this chapter continues with an overview of equal opportunities in local authorities in the 1980s and 1990s.

1.2 Local Authorities and Equal Opportunities

1.2.1 EQUAL OPPORTUNITIES IN THE 1980S

The 1980s saw the beginnings of a change in how local authorities viewed their local populations. The introduction of the 1975 Sex Discrimination Act and the 1976 Race Relations Act meant that local authorities, like other employers and service providers, now operated in a different context. In response to the demands of this legislation, and lobbying by community and women's groups, some local authorities established race relations and women's units or committees, which were intended to ensure that legislation and relevant policy (such as equal opportunities policies) were implemented. It is unclear from the literature reviewed here just how many local authorities established equal opportunities policies in the 1980s.

The equal opportunities approach to discrimination and disadvantage was often seen as London-led and, consquent to a sustained media campaign, particularly in the right-wing press, became associated with the 'loony left' and discredited (Cross et al, 1991; Solomos and Back, 1995; Young, 1997). One commentator has referred to this period of 'loony left councils' as a one of 'municipal socialism' (Randall, 1991); another has referred to the political impetus to highlight women's issues as 'municipal feminism' (Breugal and Hean, 1995). A consequence of this was that other local authorities were keen to distance themselves from what were seen as the excesses of 'loony left' councils, especially when implementing or promoting equal opportunity policies (Solomos and Back, 1995).

The equal opportunity policies instigated by local authorities in the 1980s tended to focus on women and ethnic minorities and often the approach to each was separate. For example, specialist and separate women's and race equality units were set up in some authorities, briefed to monitor policy and practice within the local authority (Breugal & Kean, 1995; Randall, 1991; Young 1997). Other local authorities implemented strategies and policies via personnel managers (Young, 1997). Either way, the implementation of equal opportunities became a specialist skill within local authorities; this has been criticised for reducing the ownership of these policies by managers and staff more generally (ibid.).

In addition to developing equal opportunity policies and new committees to monitor implementation, some local authorities instituted awareness training for their staff, on both gender and race. The training approach has been criticised for its emphasis on the individual. This emphasis removes corporate or institutional responsibility, and can thus benefit managers rather than the groups concerned, and reproduce class differences both generally and within these groups: 'The incorporation of equal opportunities policies into the bureaucratic medium of personnel practices could sometimes be felt to be a way of neutralising its potential impact and serving the needs of managers, rather than disadvantaged groups' (Bruegal & Kean, 1995: 155).

1.2.2 EQUAL OPPORTUNITIES SINCE THE 1980S

By the end of the 1980s, there was a widespread perception that local authorities had not delivered in terms of either race or gender equality, despite the often large input into policies and committees (Cross et al, 1991; Bruegal & Kean, 1995). However, this is not to imply that local authorities have abandoned equal opportunities. Recent legislative and policy changes have perhaps increased the impetus for local authorities to develop policies and strategies for equal opportunities as an employer and service provider. Local authorities now have statutory duties under the 2000 Race Relations (Amendment) Act, the 1975 Sex Discrimination Act and the 1995 Disability Discrimination Act. The three commissions with responsibilities under these pieces of legislation (Commission for Racial Equality, Disability Rights Commission and Equal Opportunities Commission) can all monitor the activities of local authorities within their particular briefs. Each of these commissions has developed structures for this monitoring process. In particular, the Commission for Racial Equality (CRE) developed a self-assessment tool for local authorities called the CRE Standard for Racial Equality (CRE Standard). This was designed to enable local authorities to measure achievement in promoting 'racial equality' in terms of five hierarchical levels (CRE, 1998). Take up of the CRE Standard was low, with just under 40 per cent of local authorities adopting it (AC 2002a). The CRE Standard has now been replaced by the Equality Standard for Local Government, developed by the Employers' Organisation with the CRE, Disability Rights Commission and Equal Opportunities Council. The new Equality Standard allows local authorities to self-assess, on a number of levels, their delivery of equality to ethnic minorities, women and disabled people.

1.2.2.1 Monitoring

It could be assumed that monitoring data could be used positively to enable local authorities to better target services and to examine the representativeness of their workforce, relative to the general local population. However, there has been little in the way of wide-scale assessment of the implementation or value of monitoring systems within local authorities. The CRE's own findings on implementation and adoption of their Race Equality Standard indicates that monitoring can be sketchy and poorly implemented (Clarke and Speeden, 2000). Although the standard relates only to ethnic minorities, findings regarding its implementation and use may be indicative of the potential problems for implementation of the Equality Standard which has now replaced it.

The CRE Standard was developed as a measurement tool through which local authorities could measure and monitor their progress towards racial equality at different levels and across the whole authority. It was launched in March 1995 in a publication aimed at local authorities called *Racial Equality Means Quality, the CRE Standard for Local Government*. The CRE Standard was designed to complement the law enforcement aspect of the CRE's work with local authorities and to facilitate local authorities' compliance with legislation (1976 Race Relations Act).

1.2.2.2 Adoption of the CRE Standard

In 1998/9 a survey was undertaken for the CRE to examine: the extent of adoption of the CRE Standard; its implementation and compliance with the Standard; the capacity of local authorities to manage equality as a quality issue and, problems with the structure of the Standard. Originally, the survey had been intended to reach a 15 per cent sample of local authorities in Britain. Eighty nine local authorities were contacted; a total of 39.3 per cent of those contacted did not participate in the survey (Clarke and Speeden, 2000). Of those local authorities which did respond to the survey, 54 per cent (30 local authorities) had adopted the CRE Standard: 'The lowest level of activity among English and Welsh authorities [surveyed] was found among metropolitan authorities outside London', leading the researchers to speculate that the CRE Standard was perceived as 'London-driven' (ibid., 16).

Clarke and Speeden questioned the high response rate their survey yielded to the question about implementation of the Standard, noting that their survey does not provide good comparative data because there is large scope for local interpretation of the Standard (ibid.). From their case study work, undertaken with ten local authorities, they found that 'There was strong evidence to show that the Standard was not consistently applied *within* local authorities and that there was both inter- and intra-departmental variation in the Standard levels that had been attained. Equalities performance was also applied unevenly within authorities' (ibid., 24, emphasis added). In terms of employment of ethnic minority people, an unspecified number of authorities participating in Clarke and Speeden's survey only applied the CRE Standard to employment and not to service delivery (ibid., 21). In terms of monitoring, the most common form found by this survey 'concerned employment, but the case studies suggest that data on the ethnic background of applicants and interviewees are collected but not used effectively in monitoring recruitment policy and practice' (ibid., 25).

Overall, the survey of use and implementation of the CRE Standard found that local authorities had experienced a 'wide variety of problems when they tried to use the Standard' (ibid., 30). The researchers attributed this to the changing framework for quality matters in local government as well as lack of familiarity with the language and terminology used by the CRE Standard for some staff involved in implementing it. They also note that 'it was evident from the survey that adoption of the Standard and publication of a racial equality statement do not necessarily lead to action' (ibid., 30). Some local authorities had also resisted implementation of the CRE Standard on the grounds of cost. However, since this survey was undertaken, the Best Value performance indicator scheme has been amended to include indicators covering adoption and implementation of the CRE Standard, ethnic minority employment and the CRE code for rented housing. Since 2002, the CRE Standard has been replaced with an Equality Standard, designed to cut across gender, disability and ethnicity. Its adoption and implementation is also measured via a Best Value performance indicator (BVPI). There are also BVPIs measuring the percentage of women in senior positions in local authorities (but no equivalent measure for ethnic minorities).

Under current relevant legislation, local authorities have responsibility to ensure equality in terms of both employment practice and service delivery. There is a specific statutory duty to promote racial equality under the new Race Relations (Amendment) Act 2000. Included in this is a requirement, effective from 31 May 2002, for public authorities to publish Race Equality Schemes (RES).

These changes in the working context for local authorities reflect the Government's commitment to a modernisation agenda for local government, which includes the promotion of a meaningful equality and diversity agenda. This is based on the assumption that local authorities which are representative and inclusive are better able to deliver satisfactorily to their local communities and will demonstrate better and more inclusive leadership styles. The White Paper *Strong Local Leadership: Quality Public Services* emphasises the need for democratic accountability, community cohesion and civic renewal. Specific mention is made of the need to recognise that 'Local areas are becoming more diverse' (2001: 13) and the need for councils to hear all voices.

1.3 The Modernisation Agenda and Equality and Diversity

1.3.1 LEADERSHIP AND MANAGEMENT

The organisational structures and culture of a local authority are important indicators of a local authority's response, and ability to respond, to the modernisation agenda. The departmental structures of a local authority, the ways in which cross-cutting issues are handled, the committee arrangements, roles of members and methods of engagement with other stakeholders may all impact significantly on the ways in which an equality and diversity agenda is operated and the resultant outcomes. Many local authorities have become more user-oriented, innovative and open to organisational and cultural change (Fox and Broussine, 2001). Leadership styles can send important messages about an authority's response to modernisation, equality and diversity. They have the potential to facilitate or close down organisational change and development. Local authorities implementing cultural and organisational changes in response to the modernisation agenda *may* also be better positioned to also address equality and diversity issues.

The response to, and management of, equality and diversity issues within local authorities has implications for leadership styles, employment practices and structures, and service procurement and delivery. Evidence from research suggests that local authorities still have advances to make in implementing equality and diversity across the range of their roles and activities. Ensuring equality and diversity in service delivery implies a need to be well-informed about service users' needs and perspectives. However, just over one third of users and carers felt that issues relating to race, culture and religion had been noted by social services staff (Audit Commission, 2002a).

1.3.2 THE FUTURE AGENDA

In terms of the future equality and diversity agenda, it is likely that local government will be working to a more complex, and perhaps comprehensive, agenda. The government may merge the three equality commissions into a single Equalities Commission (Cabinet Office, 2002). New European Union directives have also been issued in relation to Article 13 of the Treaty of Amsterdam. The Employment Directive extends anti-discrimination legislation on employment and training and covers areas such as age, disability, sexual orientation, and religion. The Race Directive covers education and the provision of goods and services (including housing), in addition to employment and training. The Equal Treatment Directive (1975) prohibits sex discrimination in employment and training; an amendment to this directive was published in 2002. The broad timetable to which the directives will be implemented in Britain is (DTI, 2002):

- Race in relation to education, goods and services, as well as employment and training by July 2003 (Race Directive);

- Sexual orientation and religion or 'belief' by December 2003 (Employment Directive);

- Disability by October 2004 (except further and higher education) (Employment Directive);

- Equal Treatment Amendment Directive late 2005;

- Age by December 2006 (Employment Directive).

These legislative changes should impact on the range of local authority activities, including employment practices, consultation with communities (including LSPs), service delivery and procurement. Legislation in relation to sex, race and disability will be amended by regulation; new legislation, in the form of regulations, will be introduced to outlaw discrimination on the grounds of age, sexual orientation and religion (ibid.).

Chapter Summary

By the 1980s, many local authorities in England had developed equal opportunities policies, partly in response to legislation and lobbying by community and women's groups. These policies tended to focus on employment practices in local authorities. By the end of the 1980s, the success of equal opportunities policies was being questioned, and they had lost some of their impetus. However, the publication of the Macpherson Report, and the enactment of new legislation (Race Relations (Amendment) Act 2000, Disability Discrimination Act 1995) lent a new impetus to equality and diversity, including in local government. The promotion of a meaningful equality and diversity agenda also forms part of the Government's commitment to modernisation in local government.

CHAPTER 2

Representation and Participation

2.1 The Typical Local Councillor

Previous investigations into local government have commented on the narrow profile and characteristics of local councillors (Maud Committee, 1967; Bains Committee, 1972, Robinson Committee, 1977; Widdicombe Committee, 1986). By the time of the last of these reports, councillors had become more diverse, partly reflecting changes in the main political parties and the Labour Party in particular, such as women-only shortlists (Brown et al, 1999). The concern with the narrow profile of councillors is based on the assumption that the more the council membership reflects the populace it serves, the more likely it can comprehend the needs and concerns of its local populace. This is not a view shared by all; some argue that substantive representation can be achieved in the absence of actual representation if a representative fulfils their obligations impartially and without prejudice (Pitkin, 1967, cited in Adolino 1998a).

Despite this progress, by the 1990s there was still an over-representation of people aged over 45 and the majority of councillors were white British men. Results from the 2001 Local Government Census (Improvement and Development Agency with the Employers' Organisation) received returns from 91.2 per cent of local authorities in England and Wales and 56.5 per cent of councillors in office after the May 2001 local elections. It demonstrates that local councillors are overwhelmingly male (71%), middle aged to elderly (86% are over 46; 30.2 per cent of men and 39.0 per cent of women councillors were over retirement age) and 'white' (only 2.5% of councillors are from visible ethnic minorities). This has changed little from the 1997 Local Government Census and in some ways the profile has consolidated; local councillors have got older, for example, perhaps indicating stasis. There are regional variations, with the older, white, male profile being more pronounced in the north of England; councillors in the north are also more likely to be disabled. There is some evidence that among new councillors there are more women. The percentage of ethnic minority councillors has declined between 1997 and 2001 (from 3.0 to 2.5 per cent).

Comparisons between the 1997 and 2001 IDeA Local Government Census show an increase in the average age of local councillors from 55.6 to 57.0 years (see Table 1, below). In contrast to this, Rao's findings suggest a slight decrease in the average age of councillors (Rao, 2000b). Councillors are also more likely to be in white-collar professions than the general population; this tendency has increased over time, so that 'councillors are more middle class than before' (Rao, 2000b: 4). This is also reflected in the increasing numbers of councillors who are retired but who are aged under retirement age (ibid.; IDeA/EO 2001) as those in white collar, middle class professions may have the option and financial ability to avail of early retirement. Overall, the profile of the typical local councillor in England clearly demonstrates a lack of representativeness in local authorities in terms of members reflecting the make up of the local population.

People in full-time employment are under-represented as councillors. This may be a reflection of the time demands of council duties, although it 'cannot be assumed, however, that the working councillor necessarily suffers adversely from his or her council involvement' in terms of their working life (Courtenay et al, 1998: 20). Although there is statutory provision for time off from work for voluntary public duties such as being a local councillor (1996 Employment Rights Act), their survey of employed councillors found variation in patterns of time taken off from work for council duties. The more senior position an employed councillor held, the more likely they were able to take time off from work for council duties; however, they were also more likely to make up this time (ibid.). This means that the burden of releasing staff for council duties was for these employers a relatively light one; however, this may mean that the time burden impacted elsewhere, for example on home life (Rao, 1999). It may also suggest why women, young people and people from ethnic minorities, as well as people in full-time employment, are under-represented as councillors: being less likely to be in senior positions, and more likely to have caring and family responsibilities, may act as a deterrent to standing or remaining a councillor. For young people in particular, the demands of building a career, and perhaps establishing a home and family, may preclude them from participation in local government as a councillor.

Employed councillors who took time off from work and who did not make it up were, in the main, still paid for this time (Courtenay et al, 1998). However, this again differs by occupational status with those employed councillors in craft, skilled manual sales or machine occupations less likely to be paid for time given to council duties which had not then been made up. Seventy seven per cent of respondents 'sometimes found it difficult to fit in their [council] duties with their work' (ibid., 42). This implies that those councillors who are in employment not only have to juggle their priorities but that they must be committed to combining work with council duties.

2.2 Participation and Interest in Local Government

2.2.1 ACTUAL REPRESENTATION

A concern bound in to the question of proportionate representation is that local authorities are not fully equipped to address the needs and concerns of the local population if elements of that population are under- or unrepresented. This approach assumes that actual representation equates with political or substantive representation. However, it can also be the case that actual representation does not result in political representation; the particular representative may wish to disassociate from the group in question and become co-opted by the majority (Adolino, 1998a). Thus while equality of opportunity may have been achieved through greater proportionate representation, equality of outcome will not have been achieved. When this happens, the faith of minority and under-represented groups in the value of representation may be undermined (ibid.). It may also be the case that political or substantive representation can be achieved without actual representation but this may lack the symbolic value of actual representation.

However, the desire for actual representation has declined with time among the electorate. In a comparison of survey work undertaken for the Maud Committee with findings from the local government component of the 1998 British Social Attitudes survey, Rao found an overall decline in the desire for councillors to be similar to survey respondents in terms of social characteristics such as age, gender, educational attainment (Rao, 1998). This decline in a desire for actual representation has been accompanied by a rise in party political voting, ie voting on the basis of party rather than individual (ibid.). Reforms in local government have led to a rise in the councillor to constituent ratio, making it less likely that councillors can get to know their constituents and enhancing the likelihood that voters will elect councillors on the basis of party representation rather than of the individual concerned (ibid.). Survey participants in the 1998 British Social Attitudes (BSA) survey also expressed a desire for councillors to prioritise the management of services (ibid.), suggesting that local government is primarily perceived as a provider of services.

2.2.2 INTEREST AND PARTICIPATION IN LOCAL GOVERNMENT

In general, the 1998 BSA survey showed that people were not interested in local government. Respondents claimed disinterest in local government as the main reason for not voting in local elections (24%), with one-fifth saying they had been too busy to vote (20%) (Chivite-Matthews and Teal, 2001). Young people were especially disinterested and perceived local government as remote from their life and interests; older people were the respondents with the most interest in and knowledge of local government (ibid.). This disinterest is likely to decrease the numbers of people wishing to be involved as councillors.

Lowndes et al undertook a survey of principal local authorities in England (to which there was an 85% response rate), complemented with case study research in eleven local authorities which involved in-depth interviews with officers and members as well as thirty discussion groups across the eleven local authorities in order to examine participation in local governance by members of the public (Lowndes et al, 2001a & b). They comment that since the mid-1990s there has been an increase in the number and range of participatory activities initiated by local councils. They found that councils used a range of participatory methods, from the traditional (attendance at council meetings by the public) to the innovative (citizens' panels and juries) (Lowndes et al, 2001a). However, efforts to enhance and encourage participation by the public were often shackled by a lack of resources, especially as it was a non-priority budget area; time commitments were also seen as a problem by their local authority interviewees (ibid.). While the interviewees generally welcomed increased participation as potentially improving council decisions and facilitating service improvements, they also saw negative outcomes from participation mechanisms. In particular, it was felt that increased participation by the public could raise unrealistic expectations, slow down decision-making processes, reduce money and resources available for other projects and initiatives, fail to enhance representativenes and encourage parochialism (ibid.). Overall, the researchers note that while there is enthusiasm for and commitment to increasing participation by the public among local authorities, the finance issue is likely to remain crucial so long as services need developing and improving (ibid.).

Local authority members and officers saw apathy among the general public as one of the biggest barriers to enhancing participation, and predicted that only self-interest was a reliable predictor of participation (ibid.). Respondents from the thirty focus groups, however, did not see self-interest as an important motivator of participation even though 'involvement with the council was mostly reactive' when it did occur (Lowndes et al, 2001b: 447). While participation for all focus group respondents hinged around the 'issues that mattered', those respondents who had not been involved in participation activities were often not well informed about what councils had responsibilities for and generally held 'overwhelmingly negative views of their local council – its services, its officers and its members' (ibid., 450). This was based on personal experiences as well as commonsense assumptions about councils (ibid.). Although focus group respondents generally made positive remarks about their willingness to be involved, the researchers note that 'people may like the idea rather than the reality of participation, mirroring the over-reporting of voting behaviour' (ibid.).

Lowndes et al note four reasons for non-participation, based on the findings from their focus group discussions, which included what they term 'ordinary people' as well as young people, activists and people who had been involved in participatory mechanisms:

(i)   Negative views of the local authority: in particular, 'there was a complete absence of positive comment about councillors' (ibid.);

(ii)   General lack of awareness of the opportunities to participate: young people and 'ordinary citizens' were often unaware of the opportunities, including long-standing methods such as attending council meetings;

(iii) Perceptions that the council was remote and unresponsive: 'a near-universal feeling within the focus groups that their local council though it 'knew best' and was ultimately unresponsive to public concerns' (ibid., 452);

(iv)   Participation in the council was only for particular types of people: this meant that people ruled themselves out from participation. While this belief might be illogical and based on prejudice, they acted as a strong deterrent to participation.

According to Lowndes et al, these barriers to participation are based as much on the focus group's perceptions of local councils, as on actual experience and knowledge. This suggests that not only are people disengaged from local government, but that they may also be actively hostile to it, believing it to be remote, unresponsive and elitist. This is compounded by the lack of knowledge about council powers and areas of activity (for example, people believed that councils should be dealing with NHS matters) and the general sense of disappointment with local councillors.

There are specific barriers deterring under-represented groups (such as women, young people and people from ethnic minorities) from participating in local government as councillors, which will be examined in more detail below. But the general disinterest in local government is likely to compound or combine with these specific barriers to make local government particularly unattractive for under-represented groups. Overall, there is a lack of people willing to stand for election to local government, indicating that it has declined in perceived importance.

In addition to the work discussed above, there is a range of literature examining the position of women councillors and councillors from ethnic minority groups. There is also some literature on participation by young people (the qualification age for becoming a councillor is 21). Some observations regarding disabled people have also been noted but generally there appears to be very little relevant literature on this particular group. There is no recent literature dealing with sexual orientation[1].

---

1   The exception, of course, being discussions of the impact of Section 28, which prohibits the promotion of homosexuality in teaching and teaching materials.

2.3 Women Councillors

2.3.1 WOMEN'S UNDER-REPRESENTATION

Women are historically under-represented in the council chamber. This under-representation was noted by the Maud Report in 1967. Since then, there have been gains, but women have not reached anything near proportionate representation. In the 35 years since the Maud Committee, there has been more than a doubling of the proportion of women elected as councillors, from 12 to 27.9 per cent, so the overall picture is of a gradual increase in the number of women councillors or 'the emergence of the woman councillor' (Rao, 2000b: 3). However, this very gradual increase means that men are still by far the majority of councillors – 71.3 per cent in 2001 (IDeA/EO, 2002). Bochel and Bochel note that this historical under-representation was not considered important until the 1970s and 1980s (Bochel and Bochel, 2000). In addition to being under-represented in terms of elected membership of councils, women are also under-represented on public bodies.

Given the timeframe of the increase in women councillors, it is clear that this change is in line with the other changes in women's position(s) in British society since the 1960s. Unlike the increasing participation in employment, though, the gains made in the council chamber are very modest and the women concerned are mainly over the age of 45 (as indeed are the majority of councillors overall). The standing of local government "seems to be a major factor in discouraging women, and especially young women" from becoming local councillors (Giddy, 2000: 8). Young women, like young men, are generally not attracted to council membership. For younger women, this is probably also related to the continued greater likelihood that women will have greater family and domestic responsibilities than do men. This observation is supported by the finding that there is proportionately more men than women councillors with pre-school and primary school age children, while the proportions of men and women councillors with secondary school age children is similar (see Table 2.1, below). This may suggest that women feel they have more time as their caring responsibilities decrease, while men do not necessarily take having children at home into consideration.

In her examination of the lack of women councillors in local government, Gill comments on the decline in interest in local government, noting that 'Low turnout at the polls goes hand in hand with a low number of people who are willing to stand as candidates in elections' (2000: 8). The lack of men willing to stand may have secured opportunities for women which would not otherwise have arisen – for example respondents in Wilford et al's research acknowledge this as a factor in their being approached for selection (1993). But given the persistently low numbers of women councillors, it has hardly opened the floodgates. Gill's explanations for the paucity of women councillors centre on the specific barriers to women's involvement: family unfriendly working practices are the biggest deterrent to women becoming councillors or remaining councillors for more than one term. This finding echoes Rao's more general observation that: 'Council membership virtually precludes a sensible combination of family and work life' (Rao, 1998: 22); given expectations about women's 'domestic duties' this may impact even more on women than men councillors. Giddy also recommends the reduction of numbers of committee meetings, their timing and even mode of meeting (web-facilitated rather than face-to-face) as possible strategies to facilitate young women in particular (2000).

However, it should be recalled that a disinterest in local government generally (Chivite-Matthews and Teal, 2001) may be reflected by low participation in local government as councillors by the general public, including women. Women, for example, are less likely to know the name of their local council than men (ibid.) suggesting that this general disinterest is more pronounced for women. There is, however, a slightly higher self-reported turnout rate for local elections by women compared to men (59 as opposed to 55 per cent) (ibid.). This indicates that those women who do become councillors may be especially motivated and interested in local government compared to other women.

2.3.2 CHARACTERISTICS OF WOMEN COUNCILLORS

Data in Table 2.1 shows that women councillors are more likely to be economically inactive than men councillors, mainly because of their greater likelihood to be full-time 'looking after home and family'; that this gap is not greater is explained by the lower number of women councillors who are retired. However, as with men councillors, there are proportionately more women councillors who are retired than engaged in any other category of economic (in)activity. This is not surprising as more than a third of women councillors in both 1997 and 2001 were aged 60 or over, 34.6 and 39.0 per cent respectively. Proportionately less men councillors were of retirement age in each year – 26.7 and 29.2 per cent respectively. This contrasts with the proportions of men councillors who were retired in 1997 and 2001 – 35.9 and 38.8 per cent respectively. This disparity indicates that some men councillors had retired early. Proportionately more women were of retirement age than described as retired; this is most likely related to the high levels of women councillors who described themselves as working full-time in the home. Young women, compared to older women, are more likely to lack the time which would enable them to participate in local government, because they are already juggling careers with home/family responsibilities (Rao, 1998).

There are small regional differences in the representation of women in local authorities in England, although there is little variation from the overall average. Slightly more women councillors than average were enumerated in the North West, South East and South West regions in 2001 (29.8, 30.2 and 30.1 compared to the average of 27.9%); of these three regions the South East and South West also had above average numbers of women councillors in 1997. There are slightly more women councillors sitting on shire district councils and English unitary councils. However, all these differences are very small. No region has proportionate, or even near proportionate, numbers of women councillors.

In both 2001 and 1997, women councillors were more likely than men councillors to be school governors, sit on public bodies or joint committees, or do other unpaid voluntary/charity work. Men councillors, on the other hand, were more likely to do casual or consultancy work. Such differences may indicate that men and women view or approach their participation as councillors in very different ways, or that they become interested in being councillors through very different routes (Briggs, 2000; Giddy, 2000). Either way, it appears from Local Government Census data that women councillors are more involved in a range of community activities than men councillors (IDeA/EO, 2001).

Table 2.1 Selected comparisons of men and women councillors, 1997 and 2001						
	All		Men		Women	
	1997	2001	1997	2001	1997	2001
Average age of councillors, years	55.6	57.0	55.8	57.3	54.8	56.4
Over retire age, % *	–	–	26.7	29.2	34.6	39.0
Economic activity, %s						
FT employment	29.6	26.8	32.9	30.2	20.7	18.2
PT employment	8.2	9.4	5.5	6.4	15.6	17.1
Self-employed	15.2	15.9	17.0	17.7	10.2	11.4
Unemployed	3.4	2.1	3.7	2.0	2.8	2.2
Total economically active	56.4	54.2	59.1	56.3	49.3	48.9
Retired	34.9	37.5	35.9	38.8	32.3	33.9
Looks after home & family	3.9	3.4	0.6	0.5	12.8	10.9
LLI/disabled	2.7	2.4	3.0	2.4	2.1	2.5
FT education	0.4	0.2	0.3	0.2	0.7	0.2
Other econ. inactive	1.5	2.4	1.0	1.8	3.0	3.8
Total economically inactive	43.4	45.9	40.8	43.7	50.9	51.3
Self-describing as disabled, %s	10.8	13.1	11.4	13.2	9.2	12.7
Occupational status, %s						
Professional/service	72.9	74.1	74.9	76.5	66.8	67.0
Non manual	13.4	14.6	9.6	10.3	25.6	27.8
Manual/craft	13.7	11.1	15.5	13.1	7.6	5.2
Sector of Employment, %s						
Local govt.	10.9	11.5	9.7	10.1	14.6	15.4
Central govt.	4.3	4.9	4.3	4.6	4.3	5.8
NHS	4.7	5.2	3.3	3.4	9.2	10.7
Other public sector	14.4	11.2	13.7	11.2	16.6	11.3
Total public sector	34.3	32.8	31.0	29.3	44.7	43.2
Voluntary sector	6.0	6.2	4.9	5.2	9.8	9.4
Private sector	59.6	61.0	64.1	65.5	45.4	47.4
Education, %s						
Degree or equivalent	32.3	32.3	32.1	32.3	33.0	32.2
No qualifications	16.7	15.9	17.7	16.5	14.1	14.2
Caring responsibilities, %s						
Any	34.1	27.7	35.4	28.3	30.7	26.2
Pre-school children	4.3	3.6	4.7	4.0	3.2	2.6
Aged 4–10	8.4	7.0	9.0	7.7	6.9	5.2
Aged 11–16	14.0	11.0	14.0	11.4	14.0	10.1
Other	17.8	14.2	18.9	14.0	15.2	14.5
Average no. years as councillor	8.9	9.3	9.4	9.8	7.6	8.0
Describes self as full-time councillor, %s	24.5	30.1	22.7	28.7	29.1	33.3

Source: Taken from Employers' Organisation tabulations of IDeA Census of councillors, 1997 & 2001.
* Percentages not calculated for all councillors because of different retirement ages for men and women.

Table 2.2 (below) compares data from four different surveys of local authority councillors in England and Wales. It shows that the percentage of new female councillors is very slightly higher than percentages of sitting councillors in either 1997 or 2001. However, the exit survey shows a higher proportion of women leavers. This matches with the lower number of average years served as a councillor for women (Table 3.1).

Table 2.2 **Percentages of Men and Women Councillors**				
	New Councillors	**Exit Survey**	**1997 Census**	**2001 Census**
Men	71.3	69.6	72.6	71.3
Women	28.7	30.4	27.3	27.9

Sources: 2000 Survey of Newly Elected Councillors, 2000 Exit Survey, and 1997 & 2001 Census of Local Government, all IDeA.

The Government set out a commitment to more local participation at the local level in its white paper *Modern Local Government: in touch with the people* (1998). But any recognition of the current barriers to achieving this and development of strategies and mechanisms to overcome them are left to local authorities themselves (Giddy, 2000). So far, there is little evidence of the political will necessary at local level to achieve this in terms of either representation or participation by women (ibid.). The lack of proportionate representation of women needs explanation. Are women deterred from being councillors by the patriarchal attitudes and behaviours described by Yule (2000, see below)? Are women less likely to be selected as candidates, or if selected, less likely to run in winnable ward? Are the voting public less likely to vote for women than men candidates – what is referred to as 'voter hostility'?

2.3.3 REASONS FOR THE LACK OF WOMEN COUNCILLORS

Bochel and Bochel suggest four possible hypotheses for women's under-representation in the council chamber (2000):

- Selector hostility: selection panels fail to select women because of their sex and/or do not select women for winnable seats because of misogynistic attitudes;

- Voter hostility: voters do not vote for women candidates, regardless of party affiliation, because they prefer men candidates;

- Female voter hostility: women voters prefer men candidates;

- Women candidates lack resources and networks: women have less party and financial resources and have less access to networks than men – this can impact on their campaigns and thus deter voters who, in principal, may be well-disposed to women candidates but not to candidates with poorly resourced and poorly supported campaigns.

These four possible explanations are presented as overlapping – so while there is no evidence to support either of the voter hostility theses, Bochel and Bochel suggest that women candidates who are perceived to lack resources or party support may be less attractive to voters (ibid.).

The authors also cite a litany of evidence which supports the perception of male bias in the political system and which deters women's participation and facilitates selector hostility to women on the grounds of sex (ibid.). They note that sex stereotypes may operate in favour of male selection candidates – men are seen as better able to govern, be leaders and cope with 'hard-end' politics (ie planning, finance). In addition to the four hypotheses put forward, Bochel and Bochel add further explanations for women's under-representation. They note that women's knowledge of the lack of efficiency and power of local government (gained as service users) may be a deterrent. More significantly, they point to the incumbency effect and its interaction with selector hostility. Incumbency is the best predictor of electoral success; the gap in electoral success between women and men narrows for incumbents. Women, however, are less likely to be selected for safe seats and thus have less opportunities to become elected and, therefore, to be incumbents (ibid.).

All participants in Gill's research saw time as a key deterrent, but time was especially seen as a barrier by women (2000). The implication is that work-life balances remain more pressing for women because they still have the main responsibility for family and domestic responsibilities. In particular, Gill suggests that for women who are already juggling work with family, council duties can be not only difficult but impossible to fit in without some form of employment release (although the 1996 Employment Rights Act provides a statutory right to release from work for public duties).

In addition to the perceived time demands of being a councillor, Gill outlines some of the other barriers to becoming or remaining a councillor, which may be specific to women. Traditional beliefs about women's behaviour and interests on the part of the general public as well as men councillors could lead to higher case work loads for women councillors, assumed to be more caring and more willing to organise entertainment events (ibid.). Obviously, this adds to the time demands of council duties. Some women respondents also believed that women were selected for wards which were perceived as having higher case loads (ibid.). Women councillors often felt that there was a lack of training and support for selected candidates generally: in particular, support from fellow women councillors was felt to be especially valuable. This was contrasted to the attitude of some men councillors who referred to their women peers as 'girls', and refused to acknowledge that this could be patronising when challenged (ibid.). These are obviously deterrents for women who are already involved at some level in local politics and, therefore, aware of these attitudes.

The greater participation of older retired women may partly be explained by Rao's finding that two thirds of women councillors surveyed did not have any children at home (2000a). However, for respondents to Rao's survey of women councillors, the difficulty of balancing domestic with council responsibilities was the most reported barrier to women's progression in local politics, cited by 74 per cent of respondents (ibid.). This underlines the fact that women remain the prime bearers of responsibility for family, regardless of any male partners' employment status. It may also suggest that for these women councillors, council membership is an important outside of the home activity to which they are prepared to commit time.

Fifty eight per cent of Rao's respondents cited women's reluctance to put themselves forward as a barrier to participation. In a study of women councillors in Northern Ireland, it was found that women considered themselves ineligible for candidature, regardless to which party they belonged (Wilford et al, 1993). This lack of confidence, however, was overcome once elected (ibid.). Rao's respondents also cited women's lack of time (40%) and men's perception of politics as a man's domain (40%) as further barriers to greater participation by women as councillors (2000a). This suggests that women who are councillors perceive themselves as having more time than women who are not councillors and/or that they find it difficult to juggle councillor duties with domestic responsibilities. Domestic responsibilities also remained an issue after election in Wilford et al's study (1993). That 40 per cent of those women councillors surveyed by Rao (base = 1,000) considered that the third largest barrier to women's participation was that men saw politics as a male domain suggests that these respondents perceived local government as an arena which was not welcoming to women's participation. In both Northern Ireland and England, women councillors stressed the importance of having a supportive partner, especially if they have children (ibid., Briggs 2000). The political parties have done little to address these barriers, and little to encourage women to stand for election to local authorities (Giddy, 2000). The prevalence of men councillors may in and of itself act as a deterrent to potential women councillors: "too many [local authorities] are seen as a male fiefdom" (ibid., 12).

2.3.4 REASONS FOR WOMEN'S INVOLVEMENT AS LOCAL COUNCILLORS

Why then do women become councillors at all? Given all the barriers and the hostility to women – sometimes blatant – it is perhaps a surprise that over a quarter of councillors are women. There is some evidence to suggest that those women who do become councillors do so for different reasons than their male peers. Women councillors in Hull, for example saw themselves as *community representatives*, and 'while possessing an interest in politics and political debate, [were] primarily concerned to protect and convey the interests of the area which they represent' (Briggs, 2000: 82). Men councillors are not necessarily perceived to be particularly interested in the case work aspect of being a councillor. This may reflect Gill's observation that women councillors felt that they had higher case loads (2000).

In case study research of two northern metropolitan district councils, significant barriers to women councillors' full participation were found (Yule, 2000).[2] By the end of her research, both authorities were Labour controlled, with one having been Conservative controlled at the start (ibid.). Both authorities had more Conservative than Labour women councillors. Authority A, initially Conservative-controlled, had more women in senior positions (party and committee) than Authority B. In terms of vertical segregation, Authority A performed better, suggesting that the more women councillors there are to choose from, the more likely women councillors will achieve positions of power within party and council. However, both authorities were similar in terms of horizontal segregation.[3] In both authorities, women were under-represented on the most powerful committees (policy and resources, finance) and those formed to deal with economic restructuring, seen as male spheres of influence and interest. In both authorities, women were over-represented on committees dealing with services and especially those which had 'a responsibility for issues associated with women's concerns' (education, social services) (Yule, 2000: 36).

Barriers which women councillors faced in these two authorities included whether or not they were part of the dominant faction within their party (ibid.). As for all councillors, being outside of the dominant group reduced their prospects of promotion. Yule also found that in both authorities there were strong patriarchal beliefs about women's skills and abilities, which then impacted on the recruitment of women councillors to front-bench positions and committees and potentially on their ability to perform if promoted:

2   Over a period of eighteen months, Yule conducted 37 semi-structured interviews; subjects were sampled by gender and ethnicity. Interviews were supplemented with observations at council and selected committee and sub-committee meetings.

3   Vertical segregation involves hierarchical divisions, so women may be less likely to achieve front-bench positions, for example; horizontal segregation involves restriction to particular areas of activity, so women may be over-represented on particular committees and under-represented on others.

These patriarchal ideologies of women's skills, abilities and interests impacted on women councillors. Women were recruited to committees that were seen to reflect women's interests; despite women not having expressed a preference for these committees and despite women's lack of policy expertise in these areas of council work (ibid., 41).

For women councillors there can be a tension between seeking individual advancement in a political career and being seen to advance women's interests more generally. This latter strategy can result in marginalisation, especially given the hostility to feminism; the former does not appear to safeguard against it, at least in Yule's two case study local authorities. Therefore, accepting positions in areas traditionally defined as within 'women's sphere of interest' may be a route which satisfies both ambitious women and traditionalists. However, it should be remembered that despite the difficulties facing women in local government, and their numerical under-representation, women are better represented, in terms of numbers, at local than national level (Briggs, 2000). Bochel and Bochel note that much of the party political focus on increasing women's representation has been at the national (including the devolved governments in Scotland and Wales) level rather than the local level (2000). This is despite findings from their survey that women prefer local or regional politics as it is more amenable to accommodating women's work-life balances, presumably because the relevant chambers and assemblies are closer to home (ibid.).

Women's lack of advancement within the two authorities studied by Yule was typically attributed to their assumed domestic responsibilities, by women as well as men (2000). These patterns were compounded by a gender-blindness which encompassed unspoken, normative beliefs about women's place in society and their abilities and thus mitigated against women's promotional prospects within both authorities and the main political parties in them. This was accompanied by an evident hostility to feminism; Yule contrasts authority A's commitment to anti-racism, which had facilitated the rapid promotion to two Asian men councillors with the lack of comparable promotion for women councillors on the basis of feminism or gender equality (ibid.). This lack of advancement may explain the higher rates of women councillors leaving (see Table 2.2); as already noted, women who become councillors are perhaps more politically motivated than women generally and their male peers, so the lack of advancement once elected may be disillusioning.

2.4 Ethnic Minority Councillors

2.4.1 UNDER-REPRESENTATION OF ETHNIC MINORITIES

Concern about the under-representation of ethnic minorities at local council level is not new. In 1981 a Home Affairs Select Committee noted that:

> It would be a welcome sign of progress if there was an increase in ethnic minority involvement in local politics…for it is by successful participation in the political system rather than through separation or special representation that the political future of Britain's ethnic minorities must lie (cited in Solomos and Back, 1995).

However, there are other concerns related to the under-representation of ethnic minority groups in English council chambers. Actual representation and participation in the political processes may be taken as indicators of integration more generally (Adolino 1998a), and status in the community or wider society. Those who feel that they have an investment in an area and that they have something to contribute may not only be more integrated themselves but may facilitate integration through their representative or symbolic role.

Estimates made in the 1980s suggested that London Borough councils had the highest proportions of ethnic minority councillors (Adolino, 1998a); this is not surprising given that nearly half of the overall ethnic minority population of Britain resides in greater London. Gains made in London in the 1980s were built upon in the 1990s (ibid.) so the level of representation of ethnic minorities on local councils has increased nationally over time. Adolino notes that comparative to Caribbean councillors, Asian councillors are over-represented as a proportion of ethnic minority councillors as a whole (ibid., 45). Women are grossly under-represented (ibid.). However, she concedes that as she has used the name method to identify ethnic minority councillors, there may be substantial under-counting of Caribbean councillors who are more likely to have 'English-sounding' names (ibid.). An additional reason to be cautious about Adolino's research is that her empirical data dates back to 1990, so changes in the 1990s are absent.

Data from the IDeA and EO Census of Local Councillors (1997 and 2001) shows that at national level there is under-representation of councillors from Caribbean, Asian and African ethnic minority groups relative to these three broad ethnic minority groups' combined population size in England (see Table 2.3, below). Other ethnic minority groups were not enumerated in these surveys, so this is not a full picture. Nevertheless, the under-representation of Caribbean, Asian and African populations is a matter of concern, especially if *actual* representation has wider import. In addition, when examined by gender, the under-representation of ethnic minority women is further highlighted: the vast majority of women councillors were white in both 1997 and 2001 (98 and 98.1%). Ethnic minority women are, therefore, grossly under-represented. As already noted, some commentators consider actual representation necessary for *political* or *substantive* representation. Others warn of the problems of reifying the identities of ethnic minority councillors so that their ethnic minority backgrounds provide the explanation for under-representation in and of themselves (Solomos and Back, 1995). Mere election of a member of a given community or population group does not guarantee representation for that community or population group (Adolino, 1998a).

Table 2.3 illustrates that not only are ethnic minority populations under-represented relative to their total population size, but that between 1997 and 2001 there has been a decrease in ethnic minority representation.[4] However, this does not really provide a full picture. In particular areas, ethnic minority representation on local councils may be much higher than the average for England and Wales. This partly reflects the geographical settlement patterns of ethnic minority populations; it also reflects the assumption held by many party officials, including selection panels, that ethnic minority representation is only important or needed in areas where 'race' is deemed to matter (Geddes, 2001).

Table 2.3 **Proportion of Ethnic Minority Councillors in England and Wales, %**		
	1997	**2001**
White	97	97.4
Ethnic Minority	3	2.5
Source: IDeA National Census of Local Authority Councillors in England and Wales, 1997 & 2001		

4   The combined populations of the Black, Indian, Pakistani and Bangladeshi groups comprise 5.6% of the total British population (NS, 2002); these ethnic minorities are mainly located in England (ONS, 1996).

2.4.2 CHARACTERISTICS OF ETHNIC MINORITY COUNCILLORS

Data from the 1997 and 2001 Census of Local Government illustrates a number of differences in the profiles of white and ethnic minority councillors (see Table 2.4, below). Ethnic minority councillors are slightly younger than white; they are also more likely to be male, suggesting that ethnic minority women are more under-represented as councillors than white women.

Table 2.4 **Selected comparisons of white and ethnic minority councillors**				
	White		Ethnic Minority	
	1997	**2001**	**1997**	**2001**
Average age, years	55.7	57.2	52.0	53.0
% Male	72.3	71.2	81.9	79.2
% Female	27.6	28.2	18.1	20.4
Economic activity, %s				
FT employment	29.1	26.4	41.8	41.3
PT employment	8.3	9.4	7.4	8.2
Self-employed	15.2	15.8	14.1	15.6
Unemployed	3.3	2.0	8.2	6.2
Total economically active	55.9	53.6	71.5	71.3
Retired	35.5	37.9	20.4	21.2
LLI/disabled	2.7	2.4	3.3	3.4
Works in the home	4.0	3.5	1.9	2.3
FT education	0.4	0.2	1.2	0.0
Other econ. inactive	1.5	2.4	1.8	1.8
Total economically inactive	44.1	46.4	28.6	28.7
Self-describing as disabled, %s	10.7	13.1	11.3	12.3
Occupational status, %s				
Professional/service	72.7	74.0	78.7	82.0
Non manual	13.6	14.8	9.3	11.5
Manual	13.7	11.3	12.0	6.5
Sector of Employment, %s				
Local govt.	10.8	11.5	12.2	12.2
Central govt.	4.3	4.8	3.8	6.7
NHS	4.6	5.1	6.1	8.9
Other public sector	14.3	11.2	17.1	14.6
Total public sector	34.0	32.6	39.2	42.4
Voluntary sector	5.7	6.2	15.0	9.7
Private sector	60.2	61.3	45.8	47.8
Education, %s				
Degree or equivalent	31.8	31.8	47.2	52.2
No qualifications	17.0	16.2	7.7	5.6
Caring responsibilities, %s				
Any	33.5	27.1	51.9	48.3
Pre-school children	4.1	3.4	7.4	8.4
4–10 years	8.0	6.7	19.4	16.6
11–16 years	13.6	20.7	24.8	22.5
Other	17.6	13.8	25.2	24.9
Average no. years councillor	8.9	9.3	7.7	7.3
Describes self as full-time councillor, %s	24.2	29.9	33.2	37.5

Source: EO tabulations of IDeA 1997 & 2001 Census of Local Government

Some of the differences between white and ethnic minority councillors seem striking, but are related to general differences between white and ethnic minority populations in Britain. Ethnic minority councillors are much more likely to be economically active than white councillors. The greater percentage of ethnic minority councillors who are either in full-time work or unemployed explain this difference in economic activity; it also reflects general population trends (NS, 2002).

Table 2.4 suggests that ethnic minority councillors may also heighten the tendency for councillors to be increasingly middle class. They are more likely to have a degree and less likely to have no qualifications than white councillors. Ethnic minority councillors are also more likely to describe their occupational status as professional/service than white. As well as being more likely to be unemployed, ethnic minority councillors are less likely to be retired, and less likely to be in manual employment. The average age for ethnic minority councillors is slightly lower than that for white councillors. This also indicates that ethnic minority councillors are less likely to have retired early compared to men councillors overall.

However, caution needs to be applied to an interpretation of these data. It may mean that those ethnic minority people who are elected as councillors are more likely to be middle class than ethnic minority people generally. In general, ethnic minority people do less well in terms of occupational outcomes than their white counterparts (Modood et al, 1997; Karn 1997). Additionally, the data are not disaggregated by ethnic group; different ethnic groups experience different levels of 'ethnic penalty' in different employment sectors (Heath and MacMahon, 1995; Modood et al, 1997; PIU, 2002). The data also only applies to three broad ethnic categories (Caribbean, Asian, African), excluding other ethnic minority groups.

2.4.3 BARRIERS TO PARTICIPATION AS COUNCILLORS

The Commission on the Future of Multi-Ethnic Britain (2000) noted concerns about the selection and treatment of black and Asian candidates. At national level, ethnic minority candidates find it difficult to be selected for winnable seats. The Commission stated: 'There is frequent disillusion among black and Asian people who have tried to make a mark by being elected to a borough, county or city council' (2000: 231). The report warns against the 'district commissioner mentality' associated with colonial rule in developing a strategy for relations with ethnic minority communities (ibid., 234). This warning implies the importance of actual representation in the absence of significant levels of cultural appreciation, acceptance and respect. Alongside this warning, it should be noted that the greatest indicator of success for an ethnic minority local election candidate is incumbency (Welch and Studlar, 1990). Ethnic minority candidates standing in 'safe' wards are as likely to be elected as 'white' candidates (Adolino, 1998a).

2.4.3.1 Election of Ethnic Minority Councillors

The election of local councillors from ethnic minority groups has the potential to send important messages of acceptance to the rest of that particular group and even to members of other ethnic groups, not least because in all cases where ethnic minority councillors have been elected, they have had to appeal to the wider electorate in order to be successful (Solomos and Back, 1995). In general, therefore, ethnic minority councillors cannot rely on any 'ethnic vote' alone in order to be elected. However, it should be noted that in a few areas the proportion of the electorate which comes from ethnic minority groups may be substantial and even significant:

The 1991 Census showed that 100 local wards had a proportion of over 43 per cent [population from ethnic minorities]. The locations and concentrations mean that black and Asian people are statistically important in the political process (ibid., 2000: 230).

Ethnic minority councillors themselves tend to believe that they have a cross-section of the electorate supporting them because they are a *party representative* rather than because they are from any specific ethnic minority group (Adolino, 1998a). In other words, ethnic minority councillors believe that party affiliation is an important factor in securing a majority vote. This suggests that voter hostility may be less of a problem than barriers at party level, such as selector hostility.

These findings echo those for women councillors – that one of the greatest barriers seems to at the selection, rather than the election, stage. The first step to becoming a local councillor is to be successful at selection stage. The limited literature available indicates that all political parties present barriers to ethnic minority members who wish to stand for election as local councillors (Fitzgerald, 1984; Solomos and Back, 1995; Adolino, 1998a). It is important to note that all three major political parties in England have local councillors who are from ethnic minority backgrounds. It was not until the 1980s that significant numbers of ethnic minority councillors could be found, some twenty to thirty years after mass immigration to Britain in some cases (Adolino, 1998a; Solomos and Back, 1995). However, there was no systematic measurement of numbers of ethnic minority councillors in the 1980s, so this is an observation.

Once elected, however, substantial barriers remain for ethnic minority candidates. As with many other first time councillors, there may be a lack of familiarity with council structures and procedures. It has been noted, however, that for ethnic minority councillors the culture and even décor (often highly formal) of council buildings may be alienating (Solomos and Back, 1995).

2.4.3.2 Actual and Substantive Representation

An assumption concerning the relationship of actual to substantive representation is that the emergence of ethnic minority representatives signals a move towards a more equitable share of political power. However, Layton-Henry found that a large proportion of ethnic minority voters did not feel that the existence of ethnic minority representatives would necessarily further their interests (1990: cited in Adolino, 1998a). This finding may tie in with that by Adolino, who interviewed ethnic minority councillors:

> Ethnic minority councillors appeared to have made a concerted effort to avoid being perceived solely as ethnic minority spokespersons, despite pressures to do so from both their ethnic minority constituents and, frequently, their white peers. Many in fact resented the assumption by their colleagues and constituents that they were only qualified to deal with ethnic minority issues and therefore made a special effort to prove their ability to work on a variety of general issues on their councils (1998a: 64).

This indicates strong tensions between ethnic minority councillors, their ethnic minority constituents and their white councillor peers regarding the role(s) which ethnic minority councillors expect and are expected to have. In her study of local government and black people in London, Marion Fitzgerald found that there were competing claims on black and Asian councillor's political loyalties, coming from the political parties and communities to which they belonged (1984)[5]. These competing demands were difficult to balance. Views

---

5   Fitzgerald uses 'black' to refer to both Caribbean and Asian groups.

from black and Asian people gathered by Fitzgerald illustrated the tensions between actual and substantive representation roles. Black and Asian councillors were generally seen as mere tokens. Interviewees raised doubts about their representativeness:

> In the course of the research, the instances of black people's suspicion of black councillors were too numerous to mention. It is safe to say that negative comments far outweighed the positive and that where anything good was said about one, it was always by way of contrast with another, or even with all the others. They were variously accused of being 'token blacks', of having 'sold out', of seeking status on the backs of black people, and as unrepresentative of their ethnic group in terms of class, their social and cultural norms and/or their political views (1984: 97).

A further problem for councillors from ethnic minority groups is that while the main political parties want black and Asian councillors or candidates to prove their anti-racist credentials they are simultaneously perceived to be a political risk (ibid., Solomos and Back, 1995). This could result in tokenism, and the selection of ethnic minority candidates for particular wards only, that is wards where it was assumed an 'ethnic vote' was to be won (Fitzgerald, 1984; Solomos and Back, 1995). Fitzgerald also suggests that such strategies could encourage ethnic minority councillors in perceiving themselves as only representing their ethnic community, although this contrasts with the views expressed by Adolino's interviewees (ibid., Adolino 1998a).

In a study of ethnic minority councillors in Birmingham City Council (BCC), Solomos and Back detail the difficulties and barriers experienced by their interviewees (1995). In particular, they note that the greater numbers of ethnic minority councillors and leaders in Birmingham in the 1980s acted to boost, rather than diminish, the power of already established white political leaders (ibid.). White politicians, and especially MPs, developed a system of patronage for ethnic community activists and councillors which served to protect their power base and deliver votes. In return for supporting and influencing 'the distribution of local resources, services and representation to state bureaucracies', white politicians could expect political support (ibid., 76).

Racialisation of black and Asian councillors and political activity was, according to Solomos and Back, widespread among white councillors (ibid.). Comments were made to the researchers about new and alien political traditions being imported which were assumed to be necessarily corrupt or semi-corrupt. Notions of corruption were particularly associated with Asian groups but were also readily extended to embrace all 'others' engaged in political processes. Within these racialised discourses, Muslim councillors were particularly 'constructed as duplicitous and inscrutable' (ibid., 99) (see also section 3.4, below). Black and Asian politicians in Birmingham were assumed to be corrupt; alongside this emerged a discourse of 'white victimhood' which developed as Asian councillors in particular stopped supporting a patronage system which was perceived to have primarily benefited white politicians and helped to maintain the privileged position of the white working class in their access to services and resources (ibid., 112).

2.4.3.3 Ethnic Minority Councillors in Birmingham

As part of their case study, Solomos and Back interviewed twenty three sitting or former councillors from ethnic minority communities. They comment that these interviewees represented 'an elite vanguard within [their] communities' with 'locally established connections and a political agenda that is associated with practical issues such as access to resources, religious needs and the provision of social welfare' (ibid., 132). These interviewees were also motivated by a desire to enhance civil rights and involvement. From these interviewees, a snapshot of the racialised political management of Birmingham City Council was developed. Black and Asian councillors were appointed to committees, but usually minor committees. Although the number of black and Asian councillors increased, as well as the individuals concerned, the number of committee places allocated to black and Asian members remained constant. The municipal culture of BCC was viewed by interviewees as alienating and even hostile. Solomos and Back comment that until recently before the time of their study, BCC had been an 'exclusively white preserve' (ibid., 148). Overall, the picture is one of a political institution which was implacably hostile to the participation of new groups which are characterised as alien, other and unentitled.

Solomos and Back observe that the position of black and Asian councillors and politicians in Birmingham was part of 'a complex struggle for political influence and representation' (ibid., 170), in which racism was mobilised in order to legitimise and maintain white hegemony. Additionally, race equality was perceived as competing with gender equality for priority to such an extent that 'gender politics can converge with racial exclusion and black empowerment collides with sexism and homophobia' (ibid., 158). Such a finding resonates with Yule's observation that in her two case study local authorities there was a lot of hostility to women councillors and feminism, but that in one two newly elected Asian men councillors had been quickly promoted (2000). The complex positioning of different and competing equalities noted by Solomos and Back is likely to have particularly marginalised women and gays from ethnic minority communities. Indeed, Solomos and Back in the whole of their study refer directly to only two women, one of whom was a white woman councillor who had an explicit antipathy to all migrant communities in Birmingham, the other of whom was an activist and presumably black or Asian although this is not clear. This indicates that at the time of their study that ethnic politics in Birmingham were not only ethnicised but strongly patriarchal.

The end result of the complex jockeying for political power and position in Birmingham was, according to Solomos and Back, neither a simple politics of accommodation on the part of black and Asian councillors (adapting to hegemonic ideologies and beliefs) nor one of progressive incorporation by the political parties (Solomos and Back, 1995). This, they argue, is not unique to Birmingham, although the particular manifestations of how this struggle is played out may be.

2.4.3.4 Reasons for Ethnic Minority Representation

Finally, Solomos and Back acknowledge the gains made by ethnic minority communities in terms of representation in the political arena. They argue that there is still a need (from the viewpoint of the late 1980s) to increase representation and acknowledge that not all ethnic groups have gained: 'The growth in political participation is the result of patterns of recruitment which have brought some communities into politics while leaving others behind' (ibid., 208), mentioning the Bangladeshi community in particular as under-represented. While they are pessimistic about the concrete gains which increased representation has delivered for ethnic minority communities, they suggest that the increase in political activism by ethnic minority communities must 'make some impact on established political parties, particularly at local level' (ibid., 209–10).

Despite the difficulties facing black and Asian people trying to be involved in mainstream politics, Fitzgerald believes that there are two important reasons for their inclusion (1984):

(i)   Racial equality depends on political parties and especially their ability to deliver effective policies. The involvement of black and Asian people in political parties, she suggests, has a sensitising effect and thus can enhance the policy process;

(ii)   The involvement of black and Asian people in mainstream leadership roles is symbolically important because it is a challenge to stereotypes, a provision of successful role models who have to act as advocates for black, Asian and white people.

However, Fitzgerald warns against unrealistic expectations of the potential achievements of black and Asian participation – the degree of influence of ordinary party members is very small.

2.4.4 REPRESENTATION, FAITH AND VISIBILITY

Representation of 'faith communities' may overlap with ethnic minorities; care should be taken not to simply equate faith with ethnicity. However, the primacy of the black/white dichotomy in Britain can pose particular difficulties for Islamic communities as the dominance of the colour/ethnicity paradigm excludes consideration of Muslim communities in the multicultural debate (Modood, 2000). The emergence of a Muslim identity, post the Rushdie affair, poses problems for all shades of opinion, as the emergence of what was once considered a religion as a publicly staged identity challenges the public/private divide which firmly places religion and religious practice in the private sphere of home and family (ibid.). This contrasts with Jews and Sikhs in Britain, whose public identities as Jews and Sikhs are perhaps more readily recognised as publicly staged identities, and which also have the protection of legislation, unlike Muslims who are not recognised under the terms of the Race Relations Act (ibid.). In particular, British Muslims have identified two specific issues as important, and which have implications for local government as a service provider and employer: the funding of religious schools for Muslims and the protection of the law from islamophobia, both issues which challenge the liberal consensus surrounding discourses of multiculturalism (as opposed to multi-faith) (ibid.).

Muslim identities pose a challenge for discourses of British multiculturalism when religion is still assumed to be a private rather than public issue: 'l'identité musulmane est perçue comme l'enfant illégitime du multiculturlisme britannique' (ibid., 52). The complex interaction between racism and islamophobia (sectarianism) suggested by Modood may partly explain the particular directing of hostility at Asian councillors, as described by Solomos and Back (1995), although, of course, not all Asian councillors are Muslim. This does not mean that there is necessarily political mobilisation of Muslim communities: in the 1990 local elections the Islamic Party of Great Britain won no seats, and came nowhere close to winning, even in Bolton and other areas where there was potentially a large voter base (Adolino, 1998a). More recently, however, the People's Justice Party has emerged as a powerful group within Birmingham City Council (Prasad, 2002). Its concerns reflect the intersecting global/local (as opposed to national) or umma/place concerns of many Muslim communities in Britain today emphasising as it does the need to find a solution to conflict in Kashmir with concerns about unemployment and housing among local Pakistani and Kashmiri communities in Birmingham (ibid.).

In addition, there are other ethnic groups which are not mentioned at all in the literature, including the Irish and Chinese groups. The Chinese population group is often omitted from statistical analyses on the grounds that, although an enumerated ethnic minority, numbers are too small. In contrast, the Irish group is the largest ethnic minority in Britain but as a white group is often omitted from analyses of ethnicity which, in the British context, tend to focus on minorities visible by skin colour (Walter, 2001; Hickman, Morgan and Walter, 2001). Both these groups, and other ethnic groups which may have significant populations in particular areas of settlement, are invisible or hidden minorities (Parker, 1995; Hickman and

Walter, 1997; Walter, 2001). Thus nothing is known about their relative representation. However, it is not unreasonable to deduce that, given the relative under-representation of Caribbean and Asian groups overall, that other ethnic minorities are similarly under-represented in local government. Indeed, any under-representation may go unnoticed given the concentration on the visible minorities.

2.5 Young People and Engagement with Local Authorities

2.5.1 YOUNG PEOPLE AND VOTING

Young people in the UK cannot vote until they reach eighteen; the qualification age to stand for election as a local councillor is twenty one. IDeA data shows not only that the average age of councillors is 57 but that it has increased over time (see Table 2.5). The numbers of councillors aged under twenty five in England and Wales are tiny, and have declined over time: 0.2 per cent in 1997 and 0.1 per cent in 2001. The very small numbers of young local councillors inevitably emphasises the predominance of older-aged councillors. It also underlines the disengagement of young people from local government.

Table 2.5 Numbers of councillors in England and Wales aged under 25 by grouping[6]		
	1997	**2001**
Men	25	16
Women	13	7
White	35	23
Ethnic minority	3	0
Disabled	3	2
Caring responsibilities	10	5
Full-time councillor	6	7
All under 25	38	23
Total, all ages	21498	21268
Source: Local Government Census, 1997 & 2001, Employers' Organization tabulations		

2.5.2 EXPLANATIONS OF YOUNG PEOPLE'S LACK OF PARTICIPATION

There is a general consensus that young people in the UK are alienated from mainstream politics (Molloy et al, 2002; Geddes and Rust, 1999; Taylor, 2001; Geddes, forthcoming). Often, concern about lack of engagement with the political mainstream tends to focus on the national rather than local level, so there is little literature about young people and local politics (Molloy et al, 2002). Young people are a key client group for local government services 'but they have relatively little say in the local policy processes which determine how services are provided' (Geddes, forthcoming). According to Mike Geddes, there are three broad reasons for involving young people in local government: 1) strengthening local democracy; 2) young people also have fundamental citizenship rights; 3) legal considerations such as the UN Covention on the Rights of the Child to which the UK acceded in 1991

---

6   The tables produced by the EO give a figure of 17 for men aged under 25 and 7 for women aged under 25; this is probably due to rounding of figures and the advice from the EO was to reduce the figure for men.

(ibid.). The disengagement of young people from local politics, however, is part of a more general trend of disinterest in local government (Geddes and Rust, 1999) and part of a wider 'crisis of participation and democratic legitimacy in local government (King and Stoker, 1996; cited in Geddes and Rust, 1999). But, as the next generation(s) of voters and political participants, the political disconnection of young people has been identified as being of particular concern (ibid.).

Explanations of young people's disinterest tend to focus on young people themselves. In a paper dealing with lack of voting in general elections, Kimberlee (2002) lists seven common explanations for low turnout by young British people (voters aged under 25), some of which blame young people for their disengagement, and others which identify broader characteristics in Britain's political system or society:

(i)   Apathy or other attitudes which are assumed to be more prevalent among young people;

(ii)   Individual characteristics which predict low turnout, such as social class. This, of course, is not unique to young people;

(iii)   Young people's lifestyles, including high levels of geographical mobility which act against them being able to participate. Kimberlee comments that if this explanation is true, then young people are experiencing higher levels of 'start-up problems' as they become independent adults than did previous generations;

(iv)   Out-dated electoral institutions which fail to engage young people and which operate in arenas unattractive to, or unfrequented by, young people – for example, current methods of registration. Kimberlee cites the M-Power electoral registration campaign for the 1997 General Election, which 'stressed that there had been insufficient effort to target and appropriately attract young people into voting; for example, [M-Power] estimated that 41 per cent of 18–34 year olds visited a rave, night club or disco at least once a month, yet this was not seen as a site of communication by electoral officials or political parties' (ibid., 88–89);

(v)   The failure of political parties to attract, and be attractive to, young people, partly-related to wariness based on past problems with youth sections but also related to the age of party members, which is increasing with time. Kimberlee argues that this wariness regarding young people has led to a narrowing of the avenues available to them for participation within political parties;

(vi)   Young people have 'adopted alternative values' in particular 'environmental and identity politics' (ibid., 90). This explanation explains the disengagement of young people from mainstream politics as attributable to a shift in values which means that young people are differently politically engaged. In particular, young people are believed to be more attracted to single issue groups;

(vii)   Generational explanations which assume that young people are 'qualitatively different to previous young generations' (ibid., 93). Young people's political disengagement is thus explained as a response to the wider societal context in which they live and have reached adulthood. This approach emphasises the difficulties faced by young people in becoming adults and posits that they are unique to the current generation of young people rather than a life-cycle event. The decline of collective identities around characteristics such as class, family, community and religion are assumed to predict a decline in political knowledge and know-how being transmitted to young people. Kimberlee sees the development of citizenship education in the national curriculum as a response to (and therefore an acceptance of) this explanation of young people's political disengagement.

Kimberlee is dismissive of explanations which locate the blame for political disengagement with young people themselves particularly because these explanations are lacking in analyses of how to address that political disengagement and their explanatory power is not sufficient to completely identify reasons for young people's failure to vote (ibid.). Nor is he convinced by life-cycle explanations or explanations which blame politicians and political structures. Rather he favours the alternative values and generational approaches which suggest that young people are politically engaged but their political interests are outside of conventional mainstream politics, and that their experiences of reaching adulthood in British society are unique to their generation, albeit with the caveat that 'neither is an adequate explanation in itself' (ibid., 96).

2.5.3 SCHEMES TO ENCOURAGE YOUNG PEOPLE'S PARTICIPATION

Some local authorities have developed specific programmes and schemes in an effort to encourage participation, as opposed to representation, by young people. The Local Government Association has published *Hear By Right*, which provides advice on strategies for involving young people in local government and illustrates this with case study examples (Wade et al, 2001). These efforts to include young people can be seen as part of the modernisation agenda, and specifically the expectation that local authorities will encourage more participation in local governance more generally (Geddes and Rust, 1999; Taylor, 2001). Assessment of these projects and their success in achieving higher participation is in its infancy, so it is unclear yet whether or not they will achieve their end goal (IPPR, 2001; Molloy et al, 2002). However, what evidence there is indicates that there is often a lack of clarity about why young people should be encouraged to participate, how much participation they should be offered, and what avenues, if any, they should be offered for influencing policy-making and decisions taken by the local authority (ibid.).

The Local Government Centre at Warwick University carried out case study research between 1995 and 1998 to assess youth participation initiatives in three local authorities (Bury MDC, Manchester CC and Wolverhampton MBC) (reported in Geddes and Rust, 1999 and Geddes, forthcoming). The research showed that in all three local authorities, the commitment to youth participation initiatives often depended on the commitment and enthusiasm of a few councillors and particular staff, raising questions about the impact of such initiatives and the overall commitment of the local authorities to young people's participation. Because initiatives for young people's participation may rely on a few 'champions', there is also the danger that if these particular members or officers leave the local authority the initiative will lose momentum or be dropped. The experiences of the young people concerned did not result in a desire to become a councillor or join a mainstream political party. The researchers conclude that although participation initiatives for young people are a growing trend, the success and reach of participatory schemes remains to be seen (Geddes and Rust, 1999).

Reporting the findings from a focus group of eight young participants (aged 15–22, six of whom were female), Taylor comments that 'young people generally felt patronised, unheard and treated as immature (2001: 123)[7]. Participants in this focus group demonstrated a lack of understanding and knowledge of the British political system and its mechanisms. However,

---

7   This was one of six focus groups organised in the West Midlands 'during the course of Summer 2000 in order to initiate discussions on the new political management arrangements and to gauge interest in and stimulate inolvement in the new structures' (Taylor, 2001: 126). See Copus, C., Stoker, G. and Taylor, F. (2000) *Consultation Guidelines*, DETR.

they also felt that despite their distance from politics, they could be encouraged to be interested. Taylor suggests that her participants were particularly interested in the loci of power. She outlines three challenges for local government in encouraging young people's participation: 1) reaching young people by making local government accessible to them; 2) designing effective communication, especially making key players more responsive to young people; 3) maintaining the interest of young people in local government (ibid.).

In 2001 the Institute for Public Policy Research and the Local Government Association sent a survey to the chief executives of all local authorities in England and Wales[8]. It asked about initiatives and activities which involved young people in local authorities' decision-making. Over three-quarters of responding local authorities claimed to be working directly with young people to involve them in their decision-making (ibid.). District councils were the least likely to involve young people but as the researchers point out 'this is perhaps to be expected, as these councils do not have responsibility for education, the youth service nor social services (ibid., 6). Overall, the survey found that there was a wide range of issues that local authorities felt appropriate for young people to be involved in but that there were issues which were widely considered inappropriate: budget setting, housing and public transport (ibid., 16).

Local authorities responding to the IPPR/LGA survey claimed to use a variety of methods to recruit young people into involvement initiatives. The most heavily used methods – youth services, existing youth and community groups, schools – are all formal local authority structures (ibid., 21). Young people who were most likely to be recruited seemed to be likely to be already involved in these three. Those young people least likely to be involved were young travellers, gay and lesbian young people and homeless young people (ibid., 20). These are all hard-to-reach groups, and may not necessarily be in contact with the particular formal structures used to recruit young people.

The survey found that youth forums and councils were particularly popular methods of involvement for local authorities (ibid., 22). Most local authorities (fifty per cent of those surveyed) were at the stage of consulting young people, rather than involving them; given Molloy et al's comments about the reluctance of councillors to listen to young people, a degree of scepticism regarding the impact of consultation is called for (2002; see below). Training for young people to help them be involved was provided by 43 per cent of survey respondents (ibid.). The report notes that 'adults may need to undertake training to improve dialogue with young people' but that this was only provided for staff by a quarter of responding authorities and only twelve per cent provided training for elected members. There was also little evaluation undertaken by local authorities of the outcomes of involvement initiatives or of what worked and why (ibid., 27). According to the report's authors, 'If authorities are to learn from the experience of involving young people in decisions, it is vital that they introduce a framework for evaluating public involvement' (ibid.).

Research examining young people's participation undertaken for the Office of the Deputy Prime Minister looked at the point of view of young people themselves (Molloy et al, 2002). This research defined young people as aged between 16 and 25. Participants were divided into two cohorts: those eligible to vote and those not. A total of ninety four young people were involved in the research, through individual and paired interviews across six local

8   This survey achieved a 55 per cent return rate.

authorities in England (ibid.). A group discussion was also held in each of the six local authority areas (ibid.). This yielded in-depth, qualitative data which was then presented to and discussed with a panel of 'experts' before the final report was produced (ibid.)[9]. The focus of the research was young people who were not participating in mainstream politics. It aimed to investigate their perceptions of politics, their interest and engagement, what influenced them and what could be done to encourage them to participate (ibid.).

Although all the participants had been recruited with the assistance of the six local authorities concerned, only six of the ninety four young people involved in the research had been involved a local authority organised participation initiative (a youth empowerment project; a regional youth parliament and; a city-wide action group) (ibid., 71). The researchers found that a particular difficulty in discussing local government with their participants was that young people often did not distinguish between local and national politics, reflecting earlier research undertaken by the National Centre for Social Research which found that young people either have no conception of politics or understand 'politics' to only mean national politics (ibid.).

A clear finding from this research was that there was a distinction between those young people who had been involved in some form of participation in local government and those who had not (ibid.). The former were more likely to have some knowledge of the purposes and functions of local government, its structures and to be positive about its role and impact. The latter group had varying responses including passivity, apathy, total lack of knowledge about local government, perceiving local government as merely a service provider (with especial reference to street cleaning and refuse collection), cynicism about politics, local government perceived as exclusive and remote, councillors as a self-serving elite, council membership as 'closed'. Many of the research participants felt that they inevitably lacked influence as young people and, for some, that they additionally lacked a voice because of negative perceptions of their background (coming from a particular area or housing estate, being poor). This was underlined by comments from some young people who had been involved in participatory structures and had found that councillors did not want to listen to them. This underlines Geddes and Rust's comment (1999) that participation in schemes for young people could actually deter participants from future engagement. The negative perception which many of these young people had of national politics was inflected in their negative opinions of local government (Molloy et al, 2002). However, lack of engagement with local politics was not a predictor for lack of engagement with national politics (ibid.).

2.6 Disabled People and Participation in Local Government

2.6.1 CHARACTERISTICS OF DISABLED COUNCILLORS

Comparing data from the 2001 and 1997 Local Government Censuses shows an overall increase in councillors voluntarily describing themselves as disabled (see Table 2.6, below). Councillors in the North were more likely to be disabled (19.8 compared to 13.1% overall). Disabled councillors were more likely to be full-time councillors: 39 compared to 30.1 per cent overall. By 2001 more white councillors were

---

9   Described as 'key policy representatives, educational advisers and representatives of other interested bodies' (Molloy et al, 2002: 9).

declaring themselves disabled than ethnic minority councillors; this may reflect a greater tendency on the part of white councillors to declare a disability in 2001, or it may be related to the small numbers of ethnic minority councillors. Similar speculations can be made

Table 2.6 Selected comparisons of all councillors with disabled councillors				
	1997		2001	
	All	Disabled	All	Disabled
Total councillors with disability	10.8		13.1	
Average age, years	55.6	59.2	57.0	58.9
Men %	72.6	76.7	71.3	72.1
Women %	27.3	23.2	27.9	27.2
White %	96.9	96.8	97.4	97.6
Ethnic minority %	3.0	3.1	2.5	2.5
Employment status, %s				
FT employment	29.6	26.8	13.1	13.2
PT employment	8.2	9.4	5.4	9.1
Self-employed	15.2	15.9	7.3	9.6
Unemployed	3.4	2.1	4.3	3.6
Total economically active	56.4	54.2	30.1	35.5
Retired	34.9	37.5	44.9	42.3
LLI/disabled	2.7	2.4	19.8	16.2
Working in the home	3.9	3.4	2.8	2.7
FT education	0.4	0.2	0.2	0.3
Other economically inactive	1.5	2.4	2.1	3.1
Total economically inactive	43.4	45.9	69.8	64.6
Occupational status, %s				
Professional service	72.9	74.1	70.0	66.2
Other non-manual	13.4	14.6	17.2	17.4
Manual	13.7	11.1	12.8	16.3
Sector of Employment, %s				
Local govt.	10.9	11.5	12.2	13.1
Central govt.	4.3	4.9	5.5	6.2
NHS	4.7	5.2	4.0	7.7
Other public sector	14.4	11.2	14.1	10.3
Total public sector	34.3	32.8	35.8	37.3
Voluntary sector	6.0	6.2	7.2	9.4
Private sector	59.6	61.0	56.9	53.2
Education, %s				
Degree or equivalent	32.3	20.4	32.3	23.8
No qualifications	16.7	27.0	15.9	23.8
Caring responsibilities, %s				
Any	34.1	31.3	27.7	27.7
Pre-school children	4.3	2.2	3.6	2.5
5–10 years	8.4	4.4	7.0	5.4
11–16	14.0	9.3	11.0	9.5
Other	17.8	21.6	14.2	17.0
Average number of years councillor	8.9	9.3	10.3	10.0
Describes self as full-time councillor %	24.5	35.0	30.1	39.0

Source: Local Government Census, 1997 and 2001, Employers' Organization tabulations

concerning the differences between men and women councillors with disabilities. Overall, disabled councillors tend to serve.

In terms of employment status, disabled councillors are (unsurprisingly) more likely than the general sample to be permanently sick or disabled; they are also more likely to be retired, a finding which matches with their higher average age. This may suggest that disabled councillors are likely to have age or work-related disabilities but this cannot be certain from the Local Government Census data. In both 1997 and 2001 disabled councillors were less likely than the total sample to be educated to degree level or equivalent; they were also ·more likely to have no qualifications. Examination of the data by government region also shows that there are higher percentages of disabled councillors in the North and North West in both 1997 and 2001 (14.7 and 13.3 per cent respectively, 1997; 19.8 and 13.6, 2001).

2.6.2 DISABLED REPRESENTATIVES

There seems to be little literature examining participation by disabled people as political representatives. This may be simply because concerns and issues in other aspects of disabled people's lives are seen as more pressing. For example, there is a particular debate about the nature of voluntary organisations – specifically whether they should be *for* or *of* disabled people (Barnes, C., 2002). The nuances have important implications for the parameters of participation within these organisations by disabled people.

However, it has been noted elsewhere that there may be important differences in participation for those with different disabilities, with wheelchair users being more readily included than those with a different impairment (Scott-Hill, 2002). Another commentator has also pointed out that participation by disabled people may involve more than mere presence if it is to be meaningful. For example, as the 'rules of engagement' (ie time allocated to speak) *may* need to be altered to facilitate some disabled people's participation (Barnes, M. 2002). Another reason for the lack of comment on the level of disabled people who are councillors may be that the overall percentage of councillors who are disabled is not much different from the average percentage of the general population who have a disability (IDeA/EO, 2001). Thus under-representation is apparently not a problem. However, given the age, gender and ethnic profile of councillors, there may be issues of representativeness within the profile of disabled councillors. It should, however, be remembered that the majority of people with a disability in the general population are older people (DRC, 2002).

2.6.3 ACCESS TO THE ELECTORAL PROCESS

For disabled people, access to the polling stations may be a significant barrier to participation in elections. In a study timed for the 2001 General Election, it was found that 69 per cent of polling stations could be considered inaccessible to disabled people (Scott and Morris, 2002). Although postal ballots are available, this may not be suitable for or wanted by everyone, including disabled people. So at the very public point of local election processes, disabled people may meet a very strong statement, in terms of lack of access to the polling station, that they have not been considered in their role as participants in an electoral process. The survey by Scope includes comments from disabled voters which suggest that this is not because of intentional discrimination but, nevertheless, can include decisions to locate a polling station in a below ground level room, when more accessible, ground-level rooms were apparently available (ibid.).

Chapter Summary

There has been little change in the socio-economic profile of councillors in England, since the Maud Report in 1967. The typical councillor is a white, retired man aged over 45. Women, ethnic minorities, young people, people in paid employment and non-professionals are all under-represented in the council chamber. The proportion of ethnic minority councillors declined after the 2001 local elections. The general disinterest in local government among voters in England is particularly reflected among young people.

The evidence indicates that some women and some ethnic minority councillors experience sexism and or racism. The strains which being a councillor place on the work-life balance may deter some women from standing for election or re-election. There is some evidence that ethnic minority candidates are more likely to be selected for wards which are perceived to have a high ethnic minority population. However, there is little evidence to show that the election of ethnic minority councillors has a positive impact on the relationship between local councils and their ethnic minority populations.

CHAPTER 3

Employment in Local Authorities

3.1 Introduction

In general, there are measurable differences in employment patterns among different sections or groups of the general population. Women are more likely to be employed in clerical, secretarial and personal service occupations, more likely to be working part-time, and are the most likely group to describes themselves as 'working in the home' (ONS, 1995). People from ethnic minority groups are more likely to experience unemployment (Modood et al, 1997; Hickman and Walter, 1997) and there is evidence to suggest that they also experience 'ethnic penalties' in employment (Heath and McMahon, 1997; PIU, 2002)[1]. Different ethnic minorities are clustered in different areas of employment; this employment segregation is also gendered within ethnic minority groups (ONS, 1996; Modood et al, 1997; Hickman and Walter, 1997). Young people (under 25) also experience higher levels of unemployment and employment change compared to older people (ONS, 2000). Disabled people are five times more likely than the able population to experience unemployment and are more likely to have no educational qualifications (DRC, 2002). Added specific barriers to employment for disabled people are: the likelihood that paid work will not necessarily cover the cost of support needs; the difficulty of securing proper support within the workplace such as specialist software and equipment; and, the perception of some employers that disabled employees are a burden (ibid.). Of course, these factors can combine, so that young people from ethnic minority backgrounds are more likely to be unemployed than young white people and men are more likely to experience long-term unemployment as their age increases (NS 2002).

3.1.1 RECRUITMENT AND RETENTION

Local authorities represent an important source of employment, across a wide range of jobs, professional and manual, both within their areas of operation and to certain population groups. For example, nearly three quarters of local authority employees are women who work part-time (EO, 2002). There is also evidence that local authorities are important employers for people from ethnic minorities (Modood, 1997). Reasons for this may include local authorities' policies on work-life balances (Birch and Purdy, 2001) and on equality policies for ethnic minority employees which may make them attractive employers compared to the private sector. Local authorities have a statutory duty to promote race equality (Race Relations (Amendment) Act, 2000) which means that all local authorities must consider relevant issues, regardless of the size of local ethnic minority populations[2]. According to the

---

1 By 'ethnic penalties' in employment is meant that occupational outcomes are, on average, less good than for a 'white' comparison group (in terms of education, class and age, for example). Ethnic minorities experience disadvantage in the labour market which cannot be attributed to factors such as education but rather to racial discrimination (see Modood et al, 1997: 144–5).

2 The 1976 Race Relations Act also imposed a duty to promote good race relations, but the qualifier 'appropriate' meant that many local authorities and other public bodies did not use this power.

Employers' Organisation, 4.2 per cent of the local government workforce meet the Disability Discrimination Act's definition of being disabled; the percentage of employees for the whole economy is 4.5 per cent (EO, 2002c). Overall, nearly one fifth of the working age population is disabled (DRC, 2002).

Nevertheless, a recent report by the Audit Commission raises concerns about recruitment and retention in public services[3]. This report was based on a large study, which included interviews with stakeholders, current and former public sector employees and eleven case studies of local initiatives dealing with recruitment and retention problems (AC, 2002b: 64). The report notes that 27 per cent of public sector employees are aged over fifty creating what it terms to be a 'demographic time bomb' (ibid.: 2).The same report also notes that the proportion of the workforce employed in public services has declined in the last twenty years, arising from the privatisation and contracting out of services (ibid.). In this regard, compulsory competitive tendering (CCT) will have impacted on the level of employees working for local authorities. This has now been replaced by Best Value but this does not mean that employment levels in local authorities will inevitably rise. However, under Best Value local authorities can ensure that contractors' equal opportunities policies, and the implementation of those policies, reach a standard with which they are satisfied. The report also notes that public sector employees are more likely than private to be on fixed-term or temporary contracts (ibid., 9). They are also more likely to be stressed by work, despite the higher satisfaction it brings (ibid.). Lower wages than in the private sector were important issues but lack of autonomy and inability to impact change were also important (ibid., 56). Overall, it appears that the public sector has lost some attractiveness and competitiveness as an employer when compared to the private sector.

3.1.2 THE BUSINESS CASE FOR DIVERSITY

Research on the 'business case for diversity' examined employers in both the public and private sector (Rutherford and Ollerearnshaw, 2002). Eighty four organisations were surveyed (a response rate of 60 per cent from the original sample frame of 140 organisations); fourteen representatives from different organisations were subsequently interviewed. Although the researchers point out that the business case for diversity was recognised across both public and private sector employers, there were differences in the drivers for equality and diversity initiatives (ibid., 7; see Table 3.1 below). In particular, public sector employers were more likely to cite personal leadership commitment, social justice and legal pressure as internal drivers (74, 67 and 63 per cent of public sector employers surveyed, respectively) (ibid.). In contrast, private sector respondents rated the business case highly (76 per cent). Public sector employers were also more likely agree that there was a link between their performance on equality and diversity and their overall business performance (87 per cent, compared to 71 per cent of private sector respondents) (ibid., 9). External factors included political climate, changing social climate and legislation: public sector employers were more likely to agree that each of these acted as drivers (ibid., 20–22).

This research also found that public sector organisations on average had had diversity and/or equality policies in place longer than private sector organisations (ibid., 17). However, length of time a policy had been in place did not have a determining effect on equality and diversity outcomes: rather, meaningful implementation 'is more likely to be determined by when

---

3   By public services is meant local government, public education, the NHS, central government, the armed forces and the police. The first three sectors employ 'nearly 80 per cent of all public sector staff' (AC, 2002b: 7).

Table 3.1 Main drivers cited for equality and diversity initiatives, public and private sector, % of survey respondents

	Public	Private
Business case	67	76
Employee pressure	39	26
Legal pressure	63	45
Political pressure	54	11
Personal leadership commitment	74	55
Social justice	67	45

Source: Rutherford and Ollearearnshaw, 2002: 7

equality and diversity became a business priority' (ibid., 34). Public sector employers were more likely to consider equality and diversity in their planning and objective setting (93 per cent, compared to 61 per cent of private sector respondents) (ibid., 27). Unsurprisingly, given the incorporation of the CRE's Equality Standard, now a general Equality Standard, into the Best Value Performance Indicators, public sector employers were more likely to engage in external measurement of their progress on equality and diversity outcomes (ibid., 34). They were also more likely than private sector employers to collect employee data (see Table 3.2, below). Public sector employers were more likely to hold managers accountable for equality and diversity outcomes (78 per cent compared to 55 per cent in the private sector) but the private sector was more likely to link this accountability to pay reflecting 'their more individual focus on accountability and...the higher emphasis on financial performance and profitability' (32 per cent compared to 24 per cent in the public sector) (ibid., 37 and 41).

Table 3.2 Employee data collected by public and private sector employers, % of survey respondents

	Public	Private
Gender	100	92
Race/ethnicity	100	84
Disability	89	66
Sexual orientation	13	5
Age	70	87
Religion	7	5
Nationality	43	63
Other	13	13
No response to question	0	5

Source: Rutherford and Ollerearnshaw, 2002: 35

The literature on local authorities as employers tends to concentrate on women and ethnic minorities. There also seems to be a bias towards considering professional rather than manual staff. This should not be taken to imply that that is the full remit of the available knowledge: as already noted, this literature review is not intended to be comprehensive and, in particular, does not cover reports by local authorities themselves or by voluntary groups. Each of these may include reports and publications which detail relevant information about other sections of local authorities' workforces such as disabled employees, for example. However, it does indicate that published academic and policy press is often silent on these issues.

3.2 Women Employees

3.2.1 THE TYPICAL EMPLOYEE

Overall, women employees comprise almost three quarters of the local government workforce (see Table 3.3, below). Many women employees work part-time (43.8 per cent), and women dominate in all the sectors across local government with the exception of services direct to the public, where men slightly outnumber women (EO, 2002). The increasing numbers of women with dependents engaged in paid work may be reflected in the emergence of the part-time female employee in local government. This reflects women's working patterns in Britain more generally, with women four times more likely than men to be in part-time rather than full-time work and disproportionately concentrated in the low pay service sector (Hinds & Jarvis, 2000). Women's greater participation in employment has not resulted in the greater sharing of child-care responsibilities (ibid.).

Table 3.3 **Number of employee jobs in local government in England, June 2001, by function and gender, % of total (N=2,003,728)**

	Male		Female		
	Full-time	Part-time	Full-time	Part-time	Total
Education – teachers	5.1	1.1	11.7	5.8	23.2
Education – other	2.0	2.0	5.3	23.5	32.8
Services direct to the public[4]	9.0	1.5	4.9	5.8	20.8
Social services	1.9	0.7	5.3	7.2	15.0
Corporate functions[5]	2.9	0.4	3.0	2.0	8.3
Totals	20.9	5.6	29.8	43.8	100

Source: Employers' Organisation, Local Government Employment Digest, May 2002: 19

[4] 'It follows that other employees in a shire district authority should be allocated to the 'services direct to the public' line. These will, broadly, include employees working in the housing, leisure and recreation, construction, engineering, planning, environmental health and refuse services. Employees in cemeteries, crematoria, markets, slaughterhouses and catering (except central office catering employees) should also go into the 'services direct to public' line. The form for larger authorities contains 'corporate functions' and 'other services direct to public' which correspond to the 'corporate functions' and 'services direct to public' lines for shire districts described above. However, in addition to these, larger authorities are asked to make separate entries for teachers and lecturers, other employees in education and employees in social services departments.' Taken from guidance notes for 2000 Local Government Employment Survey.

[5] Corporate functions: 'Council tax administration and the provision of central financial (Treasurer's) services to other services and departments. The provision of computer services to other departments and services of the authority, including systems analysts, programmers, computer operators and associated machine operators. The Chief Executive's office, including the Chief Executive and immediate support workers and Corporate Planning Employees (including corporate Best Value Officers). Central general administrative and secretarial services. Servicing committees. Central typing pools and printing and purchasing units. Electoral registration and public relations. Civil defence and emergency planning (if not employed by a separate FCD authority). Central offices' cleaning, catering and general maintenance including central offices car park attendants and porters, *unless a specific service department employs the workers*. Professional and administrative support in legal services; police prosecuting solicitors and associated support workers employed by authorities. *Prosecuting solicitors and administrative support workers employed by police authorities should be excluded from the return.* Valuation and property management. Central personnel services (including recruitment, training, industrial relations and other functions). Central management services, including O&M and work study. Offices dealing with rent including rent officers and their support workers. Registration of births, deaths and marriages. Consumer protection, including trading standards officers along with their support workers, and those concerned with weights and measures.' Taken from Guidance notes, as above.

3.2.2 REASONS FOR HIGH NUMBERS OF WOMEN IN COUNCIL EMPLOYMENT

Writing specifically about women, one commentator has noted that 'local government is widely regarded as setting good standards of practice with regard to equal opportunities' (Webb, 2001: 825). The proportion of women employees in local government has risen largely alongside the restructuring of local government, together with the shift of emphasis to more consumer-oriented service delivery and the need for cheaper but still high quality services (ibid.). Women provide the ideal workforce in these circumstances. Perrott suggests two reasons for the larger number of women employees in the public sector:

- Reasonable working-hours, family-friendly policies, improved maternity pay and equal opportunities policies are promoted in the public sector and, combined, these have made the public sector more accessible to women who wish to balance work and family commitments;

- Women's progression into occupational sectors previously dominated by men have primarily occurred as men have vacated them....Women appear to have gained access to those professions or sectors which are devalued or maybe professions have become devalued as the numbers of women increased in them.

(Perrott, 2002:22)

Local authorities often offer a range of leave and working arrangements for employees; this may be a reason why women are attracted to working in local government. The working patterns of women employed in local government are beneficial to the sector: 'The flexibility which local authorities can achieve through such non-standard working patterns is clearly associated with the representation of women in the workforce' (Geddes, M. 2001: 500). Flexitime and jobsharing are particularly widespread, being offered by 95 and 94 per cent of local authorities in 2000; part-time working is also common (Birch and Purdy, 2001). The likelihood of an authority implementing flexible working seems to increase with the number of employees; this may be because demand increases with the number of staff and/or because staff numbers enable local authorities to accommodate flexible working (ibid.). However, flexible working is less likely to be offered to manual staff, while the take up of flexible working decreases with seniority (ibid.). In addition, the way in which flexible working is offered may be gendered: flexibility is gained from women who work part-time, and men who work full-time with overtime as additional (Fagan et al, 1998).

3.2.3 WOMEN IN PROFESSIONAL OCCUPATIONS

Much of the literature on women working in local government highlights the lack of women in senior posts. Even in professional areas which are traditionally associated with women, such as education, men dominate the senior positions (Holly, 1998). Exclusionary practices which tell against women may be structural, environmental and procedural: 'long-work hours which conflicts with family life; hostile working environment; and the construction of job descriptions more suited to men' (Perrott, 2002: 22). These institutional practices may not always be apparent to those whom they benefit or may be difficult for women to challenge. The decrease in flexible working with seniority, for example, may act against women applying for senior posts or may result in women leaving senior posts because of conflicts between the work-life balance. Senior women who do not participate in the long hours culture may be labelled as less dedicated or less hard working. Of course, senior women with dependents may be in a better position, than other working women with dependents, to buy in domestic support and childcare, thus offsetting the conflicts between work and family time. Either way, this indicates that working women, including those in senior posts, gave consideration to the balance between demands of work and family life. Whether senior men have to do the same is a moot point – time and again, the literature indicates that many senior men rely on wives and partners to manage household responsibilities.

3.2.3.1 Gender-Blind Approaches

A problem for senior women, and women who aspire to senior posts, is that the career trajectory is often defined in a manner which conforms to traditionalist, patriarchal thinking. Professionalism often implies compliance with a traditional patriarchal work structure or pattern, which may be characterised as being a 'gender-blind' approach (Holly, 1998). Not only can this place demands on the work-life balance, but it places extra stresses on women who, as women, are out of place by being in senior positions or by working in preference to remaining at home. Male managers are assumed to be supported by a wife or partner: Holly comments that in her study of senior managers in local government 'the wife is clearly the resource for the male career' (ibid., 62). Female managers are assumed to have domestic responsibilities, which limit their flexibility to the job. These assumptions can affect how women and men view their working lives, as reflected in different responses by male and female staff who participated in a piece of research conducted in a single local authority:

> Every woman interviewed, with or without children, understood the need to establish the domestic context of the working life. The responses of male managers to questions about their personal circumstances varied. Some were prepared to admit to having children. Others found this line of questioning invasive and outside the remit of the interview. One senior [male] manager complained 'You're asking very personal questions. What has this to do with my work?' (Holly, 1998: 62).

These assumptions about domestic context can pose a problem for men as well as women in negotiating work-life balances; just as many women, including increasing numbers of married women, now have paid work, not all men rely on stay-at-home wives to run a household for them. The need to fulfil family obligations may be viewed as conflicting with the long work hours culture associated with senior management in local government. The tendency to schedule evening meetings (to facilitate councillors who work) may exacerbate the tensions within the work-life balance. Senior women who leave the office to fulfil family responsibilities may not have the understanding or sympathy of elected members and may find that they are generally viewed as less dedicated, less hardworking, and even less ambitious than their 'career-oriented' male peers (Fox and Broussine, 2001). This may be the case even where local authority policy is supportive of the need for work-life balance; as already noted, senior staff are more constrained in their ability to take advantage of flexible working (Birch and Purdy, 2001). Senior managers are also the most likely local government employees to work overtime and least likely to be compensated for this (ibid.).

In Holly's case study, 'many of the women interviewed realised that for women in senior management there is a continuing price to pay' (ibid., 67). Some women in less senior positions commented that they did not experience prejudice against them as women but qualified this by observing that this was because they were not in a senior position; many of these women had overheard comments about women senior managers which were 'derisory and sexual' (ibid., 68). The isolation of women in senior positions in the local authority was apparent to both the researchers and participants in the research (ibid.). All of these factors could combine to act as deterrents to women considering applying for more senior positions.

These assumptions about women's place can also affect women in less senior positions. It may be assumed that they are content with their position and would not consider applying for senior posts, especially if they are perceived to have family or caring responsibilities. For women in these positions, awareness of the lack of flexible working available to senior positions and the more traditionalist and even sexist attitudes operating may dissuade women from applying for more senior posts. The culture of management, including in local government, may reinforce gendered patterns of behaviour for men and women (Maddock, 2002). The invisibility, especially for men, of the masculine culture of management can make it difficult for changes in management and leadership styles, which could encourage and promote women into positions of leadership and management, to be effected (ibid.).

Part of the problem of heavily masculinsed cultures of management in the UK is the strict and enforced separation of public and private spheres (ibid., 15)[6]. As the burden of family and caring responsibilities still lies primarily with women, this strict public/private divide is likely to especially affect working women with dependents. This public/private divide may be especially pernicious in public institutions, including local government, which are wedded to traditional and transactional forms of management and leadership (ibid.) and which thus reinforce masculinised cultures of management and leadership. Other commentators, however, warn against the approaching management and leadership styles as male or female, as this may reinforce rather than challenge gender stereotypes (Fox and Broussine, 2001). The point is that the difficulties faced by women employed in local government are not unique to local government. However, local government is not only in a position to be a flagship example of equality practice; authorities generally have equal opportunities policies, implying that they will combat such practices.

3.2.3.2 Women Chief Executives

The recent *Room at the Top?* report examines the roles and positions of women chief executives in local government in England and Wales (ibid.). The study includes a comparative element (one focus group with men chief executives; a survey of men and women chief executives) and has a quantitative as well as qualitative element[7]. The report re-emphasises the lack of women in senior positions in local government, citing a survey of chief executives and chief officers in local government which reveals that there were 33 women chief executives and chief officers in England in 2000, ten per cent of the total (EO JNC, 2000: cited in Fox and Broussine, 2001). The most recent LGC/SOLACE survey found that just fourteen per cent of chief executives in England *and* Wales were women – an increase of just one per cent over five years (Simmons-Lewis, 2002).

In particular, Fox and Broussine detail the barriers which women chief executives face once in post. Not only are they often isolated as women in senior positions, but they also often face hostility from colleagues, including sometimes from other women, and council members (Fox and Broussine, 2001). These findings echo Maddock's observations about women being seen as 'out-of-place' in masculinised leadership roles (2002). Their findings confirm that women in local government have followed different career paths to their male peers, and that for women there was often a different emphasis on the importance of their career, compared to men, because of family commitments. Interestingly, their survey data suggested that women chief executives worked more hours than men. For many of their women respondents, it was apparent that women's careers were limited in ways different from men's.

---

6   Public spheres include the workplace and anywhere which is not 'home' or the private sphere.

7   Fox and Broussine conducted six focus groups (four for women chief executives, one for men chief executives and one for elected members); twelve in-depth interviews with women chief executives; and, a survey sent to all chief executives in England and Wales (response rate: 52.1 per cent) (ibid., 20–2).

In particular, family responsibilities and partners' careers were mentioned in this regard. These different considerations, of course, may have meant that women did not follow a linear or uninterrupted career (ibid.).

Women chief executives participating in Fox and Broussine's research commented on the difficult relationships they seem to have had with elected members. While some women chief executives felt that they had been employed to signal a commitment to change, including equal opportunities, and modernisation, this did not necessarily mean that members welcomed or wanted a woman in post (ibid.). The women respondents reported overwhelmingly negative reactions from elected members to their appointments as women chief executives. None of the women respondents felt that they were unreservedly welcomed into post (ibid.). Overall, the relationship with elected members was 'the most problematic area for women chief executives' (ibid., 61). Reported responses from colleagues were more varied, although problems with senior male colleagues and female secretarial staff were also noted. However, time was mentioned by women respondents as a factor in this, suggesting that there was a period of 'bedding in' for all concerned. It was possible for women chief executives to build better relationships with elected members and male colleagues than had initially been the case (ibid.).

These findings suggest that women chief executives' styles of leadership, management and working could be a challenge for senior male colleagues and elected members who perhaps were used to different styles. Unfortunately, although Fox and Broussine's research has a comparative element, this does not extend to examining difficulties experienced by men chief executives new to post, so it is difficult to be certain to what extent these difficulties are due to a change in person in post and/or perceived gender differences, as opposed to real gendered differences in leadership, management and working styles.

Women chief executives also raised the issue of inappropriate comments which had been made during the recruitment process and which they believed would not have applied to male candidates. Some of these comments had been made directly to women during the interview, for example questions about their ability to hold down a senior job and manage their families (ibid.). This type of comment clearly illustrates the assumption that women necessarily have primary responsibility for their families. This relates well to Holly's observation that wives were assumed to be a resource for male managers while women managers were assumed to have responsibility for dependents and domestic tasks (1998). Other comments were made outside of the interview and were subsequently communicated to women candidates; interview panel members were reported as having commented on women's dress styles, physique, and other aspects of their person and character (Fox and Broussine, 2001). Although these comments have been heard about second-hand, nevertheless they suggest strongly that women candidates for the position of chief executive may be assessed on criteria which fall completely outside of job descriptions and entirely within the realm of personal prejudices. This perception was supported by a finding from the survey of chief executives which found that women chief executives were more likely to have been recruited to local authorities which had used outside consultants in the recruitment process (ibid.). Participants in the qualitative aspect of the research felt that when women interviewees conformed to a more male interview style or where they were more honest, this was also believed to be negatively assessed: these women were seen as too hard or too naïve (ibid.). Women chief executives in the research also felt that they were under double scrutiny: once as chief executives and a second time as women (ibid.).

A recurring theme of the study was the importance of geographical location. Authorities in the north of England were perceived, by both women and men participants in the focus groups, as more negative towards women chief executives, and less inclined to promote women to senior levels (ibid.). These observations are perhaps partly borne out by the lower proportions of women in chief executives in local authorities in the north of England (ibid.; see Table 3.4 below)[8]. The general negative perceptions of women in senior positions among elected members were also believed to be more pronounced in local authorities in the north of England. This chimes with Yule's finding that in the two local authorities she studied there was overt hostility to feminism (2000).

Table 3.4 **Chief executives in England responding to survey by gender and RDA region, %s**						
RDA Region	Women		Men		Total	
	N	%	N	%	N	%
North East	0	0	11	7	11	6
North West	2	7	15	10	17	9
Yorkshire	1	3	4	3	5	3
South West	2	7	22	14	24	13
South East	9	30	27	18	36	20
West Midlands	3	10	17	11	20	11
East Midlands	3	10	19	12	22	12
East of England	6	20	20	13	26	14
London	2	7	10	7	12	7
Not stated	2	7	8	5	10	5
Totals	30	100	153	100	183	100
Source: Fox and Broussine, 2001: 153						

However, it is important to note that one finding from the survey of chief executives was that the attractions of the post of chief executive were similar for men and women respondents (Fox and Broussine, 2001). The researchers note the high proportion of women chief executives who are single, but this comes from a very small base (thirty); more robust is their finding that, in general, chief executives have fewer children than the general population (although this could be skewed by age and occupation profiles). Additionally, it appears from survey findings that the appointment of women chief executives had a subsequent positive impact on the numbers of women in senior posts in the local authorities in question (ibid.). This is counterbalanced to an extent by Fox and Broussine's finding that women senior managers were often deciding against seeking promotion to chief executive because of the difficulties they foresaw for themselves as women in that position. Many male interviewees blamed women themselves for their lack of advancement within local authorities, because not enough women were applying for senior positions. As the researchers comment: 'This view does not recognise that women's choices might be informed by anticipated inhospitable organisational cultures' (ibid., 91). Such a view fails to reflect on the male participants' admission that they generally expected their own careers and career moves to take precedence over that of partners'; rather it emphasises the patriarchal work culture of local authorities. Interestingly, women and men chief executives alike thought that women chief executives were better at balancing work and home commitments. Indeed, the men chief executives were 'somewhat in awe' of women chief executives' ability to do this (ibid., 82).

8   30 of 36 women chief executives in England and Wales responded to the survey (83.3%); 153 of 315 men responded (48.6%).

Overall, some care is needed with Fox and Broussine's research; in particular (and as is pointed out in the report), participants in their research were necessarily self-selecting. Not only that, but the research participants come from a very particular sub-group, local authority chief executives. The views and opinions reported are necessarily those of chief executives in post, thus excluding those who have left and those who have not been appointed/not applied. However, *Room at the Top?* highlights areas of concern relating to the position and experience of women chief executives. As their research included 30 of 36 women chief executives in post in England and Wales at the time, it offers a strong account of their experiences and perceptions. Certainly the research evidence reviewed here suggests that women who are chief executives must be particularly dedicated or committed to their job and especially determined to overcome barriers which include hostility to women as chief executives.

3.2.4 WOMEN IN MANUAL OCCUPATIONS

Research by the Equal Opportunities Commission also highlights issues of concern regarding women manual employees (Escott and Whitfield, 1995). This research aimed to examine if there had been a gender dimension to the impact of the introduction of compulsory competitive tendering (CCT) in certain service areas and functions of local government (ibid.). Four service areas were specifically examined: building cleaning and education catering (both with a primarily female workforce), refuse collection (primarily male) and sports and leisure (mixed). The research had an achieved sample of thirty nine local authorities, twenty nine of which were in England. This was a participation rate of 61.9 per cent from the sample frame of sixty three local authorities. The research found that all employees in the four service areas studied had been affected by the introduction of CCT but that overall there was evidence of a gendered impact which meant that, on the whole, women manual workers were disadvantaged.

3.2.4.1 Impact of Compulsory Competitive Tendering

In all the service areas except sports and leisure, staffing levels had declined either directly because of CCT or indirectly as part of the preparation for the introduction of CCT (ibid.). Refuse collection experienced high levels of staff reduction; this was in part because of preparation for CCT but also because of the introduction of new work practices and technology, which also involved capital investment (ibid.). The introduction of CCT also resulted in improved work conditions and remuneration, including better bonuses, albeit in return for greater productivity. Workers in refuse collection also retained the 'task and finish' (meaning that the day's work was over when the scheduled work was completed) system of work (ibid.).

In contrast, staffing levels, hours of work and levels of remuneration were reduced in building cleaning and education catering (ibid.). Increased productivity was demanded, but without the incentive of improved remuneration, although some new equipment was introduced. The researchers also noted the tendency for part-time workers in these areas to have flexible working imposed – a flexibility benefiting employers rather than employees (ibid.). The researchers noted that many of the women employees in the case study authorities held down more than one part-time job, bringing them above the income threshold for National Insurance contributions, often within the same local authority. There was a lack of will to recognise this, as it would mean that employers' NI contributions would apply (ibid.). Escott and Whitfield point out that this failure to link jobs took these women workers out of the contributory welfare system. The increase in benefit claims as a consequence of CCT and the changed work and remuneration systems it resulted in thus meant that there was a cost to central government, and taxpayers, through increased welfare benefit claims and reduced income tax and NI receipts (ibid.).

In both building cleaning and education catering, services dominated by women, substantial surpluses were generated for the local authorities concerned. School meals generated an overall 79 per cent surplus and building cleaning 13 per cent:

> This meant that female dominated services accounted for over 90 per cent of the surpluses generated by the case study authorities. The proportion would have been higher if the difference between part-time and full-time employment had been taken into account (Escott and Whitfield, 1995: 177).

Direct Service Organisations within local authorities remained under pressure to produce surpluses, leading the researchers to conclude that "the use made by local authorities of DSO surpluses and of the fact that some employees in the case studies have to claim benefits to top up income, means that low paid women are effectively subsidising council expenditure and council taxpayers in general" (ibid.: 178).

Leisure services, described as employing similar numbers of men and women, had generally seen improvements in employment conditions, including opportunities for training, and capital investment. Overall, changes were implemented more slowly and with mixed results. Improved facilities and services in this area were seen as essential for increasing profits (ibid.).

A further impact of CCT was the fragmentation of equal opportunities policies within local authorities. Escott and Whitfield found that few DSO managers tended to see equal opportunities policies as important and that 'many had virtually abandoned equal opportunities' (ibid., 171). Very little monitoring of workforces was undertaken within the four services studied across the case study local authorities. Monitoring was even less likely when services were provided by an external contractor. In addition, personnel or units responsible for monitoring the implementation of equal opportunities policies were often not involved in the development of CCT, so no assessment was undertaken of its impact in equal opportunities terms (ibid.). Where they were involved, their concern tended to be in terms of service delivery, rather than equality for the employees concerned (ibid.).

3.2.4.2 Introduction of Best Value

The introduction of Best Value, replacing CCT, was intended to allow local authorities to consider the wider implications of service delivery over and above pure financial cost implications. Local authorities are now mandated to ensure continuous improvement in service delivery with respect to economy, efficiency and effectiveness (Martin, 2001: 447). Equality is considered to be an implicit consideration. Best Value, therefore, has the potential to incorporate equal opportunities in ways which were prohibited by CCT – for example, local authorities may now consider a private contractor's equal opportunities policy as part of their tender, rather than price alone. However, UNISON remains sceptical about the impact of Best Value for workers noting that 'the financial constraints that councils still find themselves under AND the Best Value requirement to make a 2% efficiency saving' means that the 'pressure will be on to cut costs, possibly through attacks on pay and conditions' (UNISON, 2002b: 1, emphasis in original). It is likely that the large surpluses noted by Escott and Whitfield (1995) will remain important considerations for local authorities. This suggests that the poor working conditions of employees in cleaning and catering, for example, who are mainly women working part-time – the typical local authority employee – are unlikely to improve with the introduction of Best Value (Geddes, M., 2001). However, there is also some evidence to suggest that Best Value can mean better outputs, better quality and positive as well as negative impacts on staff (ibid.).

3.2.4.3 Unison Survey

In 2000 NOP conducted a survey of UNISON members employed by local authorities. This achieved a sample of 4,505, of which 75 per cent of respondents were women (UNISON, 2001). Within this high concentration of women in the survey sample, there was further concentration by occupational group (see Table 3.5 below) reflecting the 'high degree of ongoing occupational segregation in local government and the dependence of local councils on women to provide vital front-line services' (ibid., 51). These findings reflect the high levels of women employed by local authorities; they also partly reflect UNISON membership and possibly a greater compliance with the postal survey by women than men employees.

The UNISON survey also found that men employees worked more hours than women, but also earned more: men were 'twice as likely as women to be earning more than £228.00 a week' (ibid., 21). Ninety per cent of those working between ten and thirty four hours a week were women. However, women respondents were more positive about their working conditions and less likely to have reported job losses in their occupational area than men respondents. Men respondents to the survey were also more likely to be seeking work elsewhere. These differences are explained by the greater propensity for women to be working in 'people centred' services which means that:

> As a result they are probably likely to feel a high degree of personal commitment to clients than those in more remote, technical jobs where the immediate impact of the service is less obvious. Job satisfaction, despite high levels of privatisation in home care and vacancies in all care work, seems to be higher (ibid., 51)

An alternative explanation might infer that women are less likely to be seeking work elsewhere because, as already discussed, they are more likely than men to be fitting in work with other commitments. Thus part-time work for a local authority, which may offer flexible working patterns, may be seen as more positive and more satisfying than working for another, less flexible employer or, indeed, working full-time in the home.

Table 3.5 **Percentage of women employees by occupation in local government**	
Residential care staff	85
Library staff	87
Clerical and administration workers	86
Cleaners	85
Catering staff	89
Home carers	94
School administrators	98
School meals workers	99
Welfare assistants	93
Nursery workers	98
Voluntary sector	73
Working in private residential home	88
Total sample	75
Source: UNISON Local Government Survey 2000 (UNISON, 2001)	

3.3 Ethnic Minorities and Employment in Local Councils

3.3.1 EMPLOYMENT AND ETHNIC MONITORING

Employment of people from ethnic minorities varies considerably, with the highest ratios being in the London Boroughs (Audit Commission, 2002a). In part, this may be because London Boroughs have historically had a better record of recognising ethnic minorities; they perform better on these Best Value performance indicators (BVPIs) than other authorities (ibid.)[9]. This ties in with the greater likelihood that authorities outside of London had not adopted the CRE's Standard (Clarke and Speeden, 2000). Not only may this standard have been seen as 'London owned' but ethnic minority issues may also be seen to be 'London owned' more generally especially in areas where numbers are low or where ethnic minorities have a low profile (ibid.).

3.3.1.1 Fourth PSI Survey

The fourth Policy Studies Institute survey of ethnic minorities in Britain highlighted the differences in employment by sector between ethnic minority and white people (Modood et al, 1997). Ethnic minority people are more likely to be employed in the public than private sector (ibid.). The Audit Commission's report *Equality and Diversity* underlines findings from the PSI survey: 'Nationally, the workforce of the average council in England includes just over 3 per cent of black and ethnic minority staff. In London this figure was much higher at an average of 17 per cent' (2002a: 44). The report comments that employment rates for ethnic minorities vary widely among local authorities. Further analyses by the Audit Commission suggests that county councils and London boroughs have 'on average workforces most closely resembling the ethnic profile of their local population' (ibid., 46) while many (42 per cent) have a workforce which has less than half the numbers of employees from ethnic minorities needed to reach proportionality with the local ethnic minority population.

However, this analysis of the proportionality of the ethnic workforce relative to local population excludes district councils and authorities with less than one per cent ethnic minority population. Additionally, there is no breakdown by constituent ethnic groups, so it is impossible to know whether all ethnic minority groups are doing equally well or equally badly in terms of employment by local authorities. Despite the drawbacks in the data presented, these findings 'show that there is a significant variation in how well councils have been able to ensure that their workforce profiles reflect the black and minority ethnic communities in their local population' (ibid.). In many ways, this reflects the earlier findings of the survey on the CRE Standard (Clarke and Speeden, 2000).

3.3.1.2 Recruitment and Monitoring

During the 1980s and subsequently, most, but not all, local authorities have developed equal opportunities policies which have recognised the need to develop fair systems of recruitment and employment (Young, 1990; Randall, 1991). These policies have included recognition of the need to employ proportionate numbers of people from local ethnic minority populations. In some cases, this has been restricted to ethnic minorities enumerated by the Census; in other cases, there has been a recognition that specific ethnic minority populations, other than those enumerated by the Census or included in CRE definitions, have significance within particular geographic areas.

9   BVPI2: measures adoption of CRE Standard and level reached (now replaced by the Equality Standard); BVPI17: measures the proportion of ethnic minority staff for each local authority.

What this has meant in practice was that, until recently, there was no systematic attempt to monitor the impact and success of such policies across local authorities. Escott and Whitfield also found that 'Local government records often do not provide a breakdown of their workforce by gender or ethnicity' (1995: 152). Where ethnic monitoring did take place it was usually conducted by a central personnel department (ibid., 174). Indeed, while most if not all local authorities now engage in ethnic monitoring, there has been some scepticism about the effectiveness of monitoring to promote change. However, ethnic monitoring and data about local ethnic populations can be used to highlight problems in both employment and service delivery (see for example Simpson, 1997). However, even when a local authority is committed to monitoring, this does not mean that monitoring will be done systematically across the local authority. Nor does it mean that it will be meaningfully used once collected (for example Cross et al, 1991, examining the London Borough (LB) of Brent's ethnic monitoring; Hickman and Morgan, 1997, examining LB Lewisham's introduction of an 'Irish' category in monitoring).

The lack of monitoring is highlighted in a Local Government Management Board report, which comments that only 53 local authorities in England and Wales had reliable ethnic monitoring data (LGMB, 1998). Of this 53, fourteen were London Boroughs; but over fifty per cent of black and minority ethnic managers in the 53 local authorities with reliable ethnic monitoring data were employed in this fourteen. The report notes that this is unsurprising given ethnic minority population densities and distribution but adds that given the small number of local authorities involved, the numbers involved are likely to be an under-estimate of ethnic minority managers (ibid.).

3.3.2 ETHNIC MINORITY PROFESSIONAL EMPLOYEES

Using a sub-group of 43 of these 53 local authorities, the LGMB carried out a survey to examine the position and experiences of minority ethnic managers in local government; this was followed up with five focus groups. In total, 433 ethnic minority managers and potential managers and 93 'white' managers in local authorities returned the survey questionnaire (an overall response rate of 25.6%). Analysis of the survey returns found that ethnic minority respondents were generally younger than their white counterparts, with only 32 per cent aged over 40, compared to 69 per cent. Length of service in local government was also different, and ethnic minority mangers serving an average of ten years to white managers 17.5 years, although this was affected by 'a disproportionate number of very long-serving white staff' (ibid., 15). This cluster of long-serving white staff is also used by the report's authors to explain the differential spread across the staff hierarchy, and ethnic minority managers more evenly spread across it than white managers. It may also explain the difference in outside experience to local government, with 45 per cent of ethnic minority managers having outside experience to white managers' 17.5 per cent. Broadly speaking, white managers also reported having wider ranging management responsibilities and managed more staff than their ethnic minority counterparts (ibid.).

Women respondents as a whole were more likely to have taken career breaks, reflecting the continued higher responsibility laid on women for home and family obligations. In the survey, ethnic minority men were the most likely to say they aspired to being a chief executive or chief officer; ethnic minority women were more likely to aspire to a principal officer post or work outside of local government. In contrast, white men were the least interested in a career outside of local government (ibid.).

Findings from the focus groups carried out for this research suggested that there were four key issues for ethnic minority managers in local government in England and Wales (ibid., 51):

- The need for a development programme for ethnic minority managers, although concern was raised about ghettoising black and ethnic minority managers;

- Getting to the top of the management hierarchy;

- Access to resources and the need for support to pursue development;

- Transforming local authorities.

Another concern raised in the focus groups was the significant role elected members were perceived as playing in the selection of senior officers, often 'to the detriment of black and other minority ethnic groups' (ibid., 55). Ethnic minority focus group participants also expressed ambivalence about becoming chief executives, despite the survey's findings of high levels of aspiration to this post among black and ethnic minority respondents. In particular, fears were expressed about becoming isolated as they progressed up the hierarchical scale.

These findings mirror some of those on women chief executives. The shorter length of time served in local government reflects the more varied careers of ethnic minority managers, similar to that noted for women chief executives by Fox and Broussine (2001). This shorter length of time served by ethnic minority managers is underlined by the cluster of white managers who were 'very long serving' (LGMB 1998, 15). Perceptions that elected members discriminated against ethnic minority applicants in recruitment processes and fears of becoming isolated also reflect findings reported by Fox and Broussine in their study of women chief executives (2001).

The most recent survey of chief executives in England and Wales shows that only five per cent of chief executives identify themselves as coming from an ethnic minority background other than white British (Table 3.6, below):

Table 3.6 Ethnic background of Local Authority Chief Executives, %s	
Black British	0.6
Black African/Caribbean	0.3
Asian	0.6
Irish	0.6
White European	2.7
White British	95.0
Source: LGC/SOLACE survey, reported in Simmons-Lewis, 2002	

3.3.3 ETHNIC MINORITY MANUAL EMPLOYEES

In their research for the Equal Opportunities Commission, Escott and Whitfield noted the low numbers of ethnic minority employees in the thirty nine local authorities they studied (1995). Their research was designed to examine the impact of compulsory competitive tendering on women employees in manual work. In particular, it examined the impact of CCT on four service areas: building cleaning, educational catering, sport and leisure, and refuse collection. The authors raised concerns about the position of ethnic minority workers in their case study local authorities, noting that black women were employed in catering, cleaning (female dominated areas) and sports and leisure. In contrast, there was a very low level of black employment in the traditionally male dominated area of refuse collection (ibid.). In 60 per cent of these local authorities 'black workers are under-represented compared to their share of the population in both male and female dominated services....Where black workers are employed, they often remain at the bottom of the manual grades and concentrated in the lowest paid, lowest status work' (ibid., 152).

3.3.4 ETHNIC MINORITIES, EMPLOYMENT BARRIERS

Concerns have been raised elsewhere about the employment of ethnic minority staff in the public sector, including local authorities (Modood et al, 1997). Black managers working in local authorities reported that they believed they faced more hurdles than their white counterparts in moving up the career ladder, including local authorities which were 'not ready' for black chief executives and 'gatekeeping' (impeding access, often based on prejudice) by elected members (Fair, 1997). Responses to the Macpherson report by some local authorities included commitments to tackle institutional racism, but many did not address this at all (Palmer, 2000)[10]. Local government is still vulnerable to charges of racial discrimination which, as one commentator writes 'is remarkable when you recall that it was local government that pioneered anti-racist policies during the 1980s' (Fair, 1999: 33). Elsewhere cynicism has been aired regarding the ability and commitment of local authorities to promote a post-Macpherson agenda (Bourne, 2001). In contrast, however, the comparative success of local government in promoting managers from ethnic minority populations has been cited as an exemplar for the NHS in an article drawing on the same LGMB study quoted by Fair (Tate, 1998).

There are indicators that anti-racism policies and efforts to challenge institutional racism have not always been met with enthusiasm by local authorities: the CRE's leadership challenge was grossly under-subscribed, attracting only three local authorities to the scheme (Fair, 1999). Fair also notes that where ethnic minority population are perceived to be small, personnel managers may use the working assumption that there is *de facto* no problem (ibid.). He also asserts that the overall lack of progress for ethnic minority managers in local authorities indicates that there is a glass ceiling for ethnic minority employees, although this is not unique to local authorities: 'no public body has made any real progress in moving black people up the management ladder and, in areas of low ethnic minority populations, many pretend that ethnic minorities do not exist' (ibid., 34).

Chapter Summary

Just under seventy five per cent of all local authority employees in England are women, and the majority of these work part-time. Many are employed in manual and non-professional jobs. Part-time women manual workers in particular tend to be neglected in equal opportunities policies. Women and people from ethnic minorities are both under-represented at senior management level in local authorities in England. The literature identifies a 'glass ceiling' for women and ethnic minority employees. For those women and ethnic minority managers in local government, there are more barriers to climbing further up the career ladder than for their male and white counterparts, including direct and indirect discrimination from colleagues and councillors. Women and ethnic minority managers aspire to reaching the top (chief executive) but also worry that this would result in isolation and lack of support as their career progressed. Some avoid seeking promotion because of this and because they are aware of the bad experiences of those women and ethnic minority employees who have secured promotion.

---

10 The Macpherson report is properly referred to as *The Stephen Lawrence Inquiry Report*. It is the published report of a public inquiry, led by Sir William Macpherson, into the police investigation of the murder of Stephen Lawrence, a young black man. One of the findings of the inquiry was that the investigation was affected by institutional racism in the Metropolitan Police Service. No-one has been convicted of the murder of Stephen Lawrence.

CHAPTER 4
Local Authorities and Services

4.1 Introduction

Local authorities are an important deliverer of services to the local communities they serve. As a major provider of services, either directly or indirectly through sub-contracting, local government has an important role in the promotion of equality and diversity. Over the last twenty years, there have been a number of changes in how these services have been developed and delivered. In particular, successive governments have encouraged partnership working with both the private sector and voluntary and community sectors. In terms of local government service delivery, one commentator has said that 'the responsibility for services such as training, local economic development and urban regeneration, schools, further and higher education, housing and policy has shifted to quangos' (Sperling, 1998: 472). However, while there may appear to be scepticism regarding the capacity of local government in service delivery, local government nevertheless remains an important player (Geddes and Newman, 2002).

Traditionally, services were delivered in-house by local authorities; the introduction of Compulsory Competitive Tendering (CCT) meant that for particular services, local authorities were obliged to seek tenders and select the most cost effective bid for service provision. CCT has now been replaced by the Best Value regime. This still incorporates an obligation to seek value for money savings in service delivery, but gives local authorities a wider range of considerations in judging tenders, including 'social and quality related criteria' (Bailey and Jones, 2001: 1). The Best Value regime includes offering a greater 'voice' to service users in the determination of adequate services; thus the Best Value surveys include measurements of user satisfaction, as well as other 'performance indicators'.

While the Best Value Performance Indicators (BVPIs) may go some way in throwing light on this topic (see section 4.4), there is a dearth of information about the effectiveness of local government in managing services and procurement in order to deliver policy aspirations around equality and diversity. What little literature there is, is mostly now rather old. Cross et al's examination of the London Borough of Brent in the late 1980s indicated that while there was a commitment to equal opportunities, this was not necessarily mainstreamed across the council's activities (1991). Similarly, Ousley's (1990) discussion of equal opportunities – positioned as both critic and insider/practitioner – highlighted the shallowness of implementation and the resistance to institutional change. That equality and diversity are merely paper policies which lack measurement in terms of services and outcomes remains a concern for more recent commentators (Tomlins, 1999: 25).

Although this section aims to look at service delivery, it is beyond the scope of this literature review to examine the individual sectors within local government. However, it should be noted that there is a range of literature, particularly dealing with ethnic minorities and individual services. This has partly come about because of the introduction of an ethnic category question in the 1991 Census, which for the first time provided a large-scale dataset with sufficient numbers of ethnic minority respondents[1]. This data illustrated the gap between the enumerated ethnic minorities and the 'white' population on socio-economic measures, a gap which generally widened when Irish-born respondents were taken out of the 'white' category (Hickman and Walter, 1997; Owen, 1995). Much of the work of that period, post-1991 Census, has been characterised as concerning itself with mapping indices of disadvantage and deprivation in order to influence policy and improve delivery in specific services which match to indices of deprivation (eg housing) (Tomlins, 1999). While this has been valuable in providing a picture of discrimination and disadvantage among the ethnic minority population, this is only a partial picture in terms of equality and diversity, and throws no light on how well or otherwise local authorities have responded to this type of data.

4.2 Demography and Service Delivery

One of the issues inflected in service delivery is the perception of the local population for which services are ostensibly designed. How that population is structured and where different sub-groups are located, and beliefs about structure and location, may not match (Solomos and Back, 1995). This can affect service design in such a way that it only delivers to certain groups within the local population. Collier, in advancing the case for incorporating equality in service delivery, comments that so-called minority groups within the population account for 70 per cent of the population, allowing for overlaps (1998)[2]. Thus minority issues and equality in service delivery can be reformulated as an issue which impacts on a large section of a given population.

Nevertheless, there are demographic differences between some population groups, which may have implications for managing equality in service delivery. In terms of geographic location, ethnic minorities, gays and lesbians and some faith communities are more likely to be settled in large urban areas than elsewhere. A consequence of this is that while some larger, urban authorities may have developed appropriate services for these groups, other authorities may believe that it is not necessary for them to do so as numbers are small and/or unknown. Women, older people, disabled people and young people are found in all local authority areas, although there may be differences in proportions for some of these groups (for example, higher numbers of older people in towns on the south coast). For ethnic minority populations, mainly located in urban areas, this differential geographical distribution reflects migration and settlement patterns, and may subsequently have been reinforced by poverty, racism (including in the allocation of housing) or fear of racism, and preference to live near members of one's own ethnic group (Lakey, 1997). Regardless, ethnic minority populations are still a minority population even in areas where there are higher numbers (ibid.). Ethnic minority populations also have a younger age structure to that of the white British population (National Statistics 2002).

Data from the 1991 Census illustrates both the patterns of geographical settlement in urban settings and the different settlement patterns by ethnic group (Lakey, 1997: 186). This can

---

1   Although the General Household Survey and the Labour Force Survey now also include an ethnic category question, their smaller sample size and the method of sampling – using the Postcode Address File or PAF – can mean that numbers of ethnic minority respondents are too low to provide meaningful data unless several years' of survey data are combined. This combining of different years of data can result in other problems – comparable questions may not have been asked, changes over time may make comparisons difficult.

2   This is based on a calculation which begins with women constituting 52 per cent of the population. Women, in this line of thought, are a political minority if not a numerical one.

mean that local populations of ethnic minorities and the reasons for settlement in a particular areas are specific. This has been encouraged by chain migration practices, and by local employment opportunities (eg Asian workers were specifically recruited to work in cotton mills in Lancashire in the 1970s) (ibid., 184–6). Within a given local authority area, therefore, different ethnic minorities may or may not be present; they may also be differentially spatially placed within the authority's geographical area. It is important to note, however, that real settlement patterns as measured by the census may not match local beliefs about settlement patterns, what Solomos and Back refer to as an imagined racial geography of an area (1995). Some ethnic minority populations may also be more 'visible' than others; this may be reflected in local authority policy and service management and delivery. This 'visibility' is unrelated to skin colour.

The importance of this differential settlement and different population structure is that it has been increasingly recognised that different ethnic minority groups experience different disadvantages and have differing social and cultural needs (Berthoud et al, 2001: 8). Local authorities have different ethnic minority populations in their catchment areas and different concentrations of ethnic minority populations (ONS 1996). Forty five per cent of the total enumerated ethnic minority population lived in London in 1991 but beyond that different ethnic minority groups have differing patterns of settlement or geographic distribution (ibid.). Given the key role of local authorities in the design and delivery of services, this can be an important area of interaction between local authorities and ethnic minority populations.

For gays and lesbians, the existence of 'visible, well-developed gay communities' in some cities may attract gays and lesbians, acting on the belief that such urban areas are preferable to smaller towns and rural areas where intolerance can be high (Dunne et al, 2002). Some faith groups, such as those particularly associated with ethnic minorities, may be mainly urban based, as in the case of Islam. However, this does not mean that some local authorities should plan their services on the basis that particular sub-groups are numerically low in local populations. Where ethnic minority populations are small, there is some reason to believe that the incidences of racial attacks are higher, for example, suggesting that these people are more vulnerable and isolated than ethnic minority populations in urban areas (Commission on the Future of Multi-Ethnic Britain, 2000).

4.3 Modernisation and Equality in Service Delivery

The landscape in which equality and diversity are delivered in local government in England has changed. The introduction of the Race Relations (Amendment) Act 2000 places a statutory duty on local government (and other institutions) to promote race equality. The Macpherson report on the inquiry into the death of Stephen Lawrence and its raising of the issue of 'institutional racism' also spurred local authorities, among others, to re-examine their policies and procedures with regard to equality for ethnic minority people (Bailey and Jones, 2001). The Commission for Racial Equality issued a self-measurement tool through which local authorities could assess their implementation of 'racial equality'. By 1999/2000, half of all English councils had adopted the CRE Standard (AC 2002a). However, by 2000/2001, just over 40 per cent of English councils assessed themselves as not having reaching level one (the first level) of the CRE Standard (ibid.). The development of a BVPI to measure the adoption of and level reached within the CRE Standard, has provided a measure of 'racial equality' which covers the full remit of local authority activity across

England. The Equality Standard, similarly to be measured by BVPI 2 in the 2003 Best Value surveys, has now replaced the CRE Standard. A flaw, however, is that both these standards rely on self-assessment by local authorities, and so are dependent on the existence of expertise in equalities within local government. It remains to be seen whether there will be higher rates of adoption for the Equality Standard.

4.3.1 COMMUNITY GOVERNANCE

Under the new modernisation agenda, 'community governance' is central (Osborne and McLaughlin, 2002: 57). Local authorities are now required to develop strategies for their local communities in consultation with the public and partner organisations under the terms of the Local Government Act 2000. This can include consultation with local voluntary and community organisations, some of which may specifically serve hard-to-reach and socially excluded groups. The desire of local government to involve voluntary and community organisations (VCOs) in local service delivery is not new however (Foley and Martin, 2000; Foley, 2002; Osborne and McLaughlin, 2002). Some commentators remain sceptical about the level of involvement of VCOs in local service delivery, commenting on questions of adequate resourcing for VCOs in order to deliver services, proper and meaningful involvement of VCOs in policy development and service planning as well as simple service delivery, and the problem of 'mainstreaming' which may, some commentators suggest, actually further marginalise socially excluded groups (ibid.; Foley and Martin, 2000; Thomas and Lo Piccolo, 2000). For example, black and ethnic minority organisations, which tend to be small (with the exception of relevant housing associations), have found it difficult to compete within the contract culture engendered by CCT while larger, mainstream agencies which have secured funding 'rarely have any black representation' (McLeod et al, 2001: 6). This can mean that the black and minority ethnic voluntary sector is 'squeezed out of the process of policy development and service delivery' (ibid., 8). However, it should also be noted that local authorities remain important, and often primary, sources of funding for black and minority ethnic voluntary sector organisations (ibid., 36).

In addition to these concerns, it is not yet clear that the increased impetus to involve communities and VCOs will result in better designed and delivered local services (ibid.). This is at least in part because this involvement is still relatively new, but also because it is not yet apparent that the VCO sector can move at the quick pace of change envisaged by central government (Foley and Martin, 2000). Additionally, there are concerns about the shape of community-based approaches and particularly the assumption of geographically based community cohesion that these approaches can imply (ibid.). Specifically, Foley and Martin note that: an area-based approach may be unsuited in an era when increasing numbers of people belong to non-geographic communities; the approach does not recognise that communities may be deeply fragmented and in conflict; nor does it recognise that some service users may favour services which enhance rather than combat social exclusion (ibid.). This further complicates the question of geographical location discussed earlier (in 4.2). Their concerns imply that there are equality issues to be addressed within this framework of increased community participation and local service delivery. These findings are complemented by Dibben and Bartlett's finding that when local communities were consulted in four case study local authorities that the best results, that is a successful outcome in terms of changes to services and empowerment of service users who were consulted, were achieved when council officers were clear about what they wanted to consult on and when their desired outcomes were matched by the outcomes from the consultation process (2001). In other words, consultation was at its most successful when it 'did not threaten to undermine the position or power base of officers or members' (ibid., 57).

4.3.2 SOCIAL EXCLUSION

The emphasis from central government on tackling social exclusion has also led to a shift in emphasis to service delivery at the local level (Pitts and Hope, 1997). According to some commentators, this shift in emphasis implies a programme of community empowerment: 'Good local management implies high performance not only in managing local services so that they satisfy customers and taxpayers but also in enabling local communities to solves their own problems and to create better futures for their stakeholders' (Bovaird and Löffler, 2002: 9). Reducing social exclusion implies that services should meet the needs of the most disadvantaged in order to ameliorate or alleviate that disadvantage (Geddes and Newman, 2002: 4). But there is scant evidence that local authorities have moved to a position of implementing equality and diversity in order to promote social inclusion. For example, a study by Muddiman et al (2000) of public library service provision illustrates how local authority equal opportunity policies can be patchily implemented across service areas. They suggest that there is a need for guidance about which groups, neighbourhoods or communities policies are designed for – this is not an argument for greater control or direction from central government but for ownership within local government of policies and comprehension of their implications and intended remit.

An outcome of the focus on social exclusion has been a concentration on housing and areas of deprivation. A plethora of 'area-based initiatives' were developed in an effort to reduce poverty and deprivation in the worst wards and on the worst housing estates. However, this brings its own problems. The sheer volume of new 'area based initiatives' may negatively impact on local authority's capacity to implement change (Geddes and Newman, 2002; Geddes and Root, 2000), although the need to rationalise the number of schemes has now been recognised (RCU 2002). The focus on areas of severe deprivation may also mean that areas which are deprived or struggling may 'miss out' because they are not deprived enough. Additionally, the focus on the worst housing estates has been criticised because it inevitably centres on local authority housing estates, thus excluding other areas and excluding ethnic minority people who are less likely than the majority population to be living in local authority housing – although when they do, there is some evidence to suggest that they are more likely to have been allocated lower quality housing (Tomlins, 1999). It also excludes those who have bought their homes: for example, there are above average rates of owner occupation in Indian, Pakistani and African Asian households, although the housing concerned may be of poor quality (Lakey, 1997:199).

4.3.3 EQUALITY IN SERVICE DELIVERY

Equalities work in local authorities has in the past tended to concentrate on employment issues (Collier, 1998: 1; see Chapter 3 in this review). There is relatively little literature examining services in a holistic way. However, Rohan Collier's (1998) *Equality in Managing Service Delivery* provides an overview of equality in service delivery plus a guide to delivering equality through services from the perspective of a practitioner[3]. Much of the rest of this section draws on this source.

According to Collier, in the 1980s, equal opportunities in services tended to be detached and piecemeal, and therefore not integrated into corporate strategies; the emphasis tended to be

3 Collier worked for LB Croydon and LB Hounslow: 'Most of the thinking behind this book and its contents were developed as part of my work in these two organisations. Much of the material used in the book is reproduced with their permission' (1998: viii). Also drawn on are examples from LB Haringey and Reading Council, perhaps suggesting a south east England focus.

on providing separate services for different groups, rather than mainstreaming equalities (ibid., 4). Equalities was seen as an add-on rather than an integral part of service delivery and was, therefore 'vulnerable and easily dropped when cuts were called for' (ibid.). However, by the 1990s, there was a shift with equalities work becoming more strategic, and this included a shift towards empowerment of front-line staff and towards delivery of equality through services, partly arising out of the emphasis on service users as consumers (ibid., 6). Collier notes that while the increased emphasis on consumer choice did lead to changes in services which enhanced user experience, this approach was limited because it only dealt with current, rather than potential, customers and was particularly weak as an approach in public services 'where choice may be limited by factors such as poverty, illiteracy or the inability to speak English' (ibid., 7). Monitoring service users is advocated as a method to identify not only who uses services but who is under using or not using services (ibid., 101).

Drawing on Beck's concept of the 'risk society' (1992), Collier suggests that increasing choice for service users also increases risk-taking and therefore can be disempowering rather than empowering (ibid., 8). She argues that trust is as important, or even more important, in service delivery in the public sector, not least because parts of it, such as planning, do not serve individuals but communities (ibid., 9). If this is the case, then the issue of trust feeds back into how the local authority, including councillors and officers, is viewed. If a local authority is poorly perceived, then it may not be trusted to deliver quality services. Lack of trust by particular groups may deter or reduce their use of services.

Collier asserts that a quality approach to services does not necessarily lead to equality in service delivery: 'there cannot be high quality services without equality' (ibid. 19). This forms part of an argument for the business case for equalities. Not only do minority groups compose 70 per cent of the population but, according to Collier, incorporating equality in service delivery: increases the customer base and improves public image/avoids adverse publicity (ibid., 24–7). Collier adds that both litigation and discrimination are expensive and thus incorporating equality saves money – discrimination can be expensive because it may result in separate or special services having to be provided as a consequence (ibid.). Equality in service delivery is not about equal services but appropriate services according to different needs (ibid., 29). Providing appropriate and equality-based services is more effective: it enhances accessibility and take up and improves service outcomes (ibid., 107).

In arguments for the business case for equality, it is noticeable that the issue of employees and their representativeness is seen as key (ibid.; Rutherford and Ollerearnshaw, 2002). This approach suggests that if employees are similar to customers and service users then employees are more likely to be responsive to needs and 'Customers will be more likely to feel that they are being treated equally if the staff serving them include people who are similar to themselves' (Collier, 1998: 22). A problem with this approach is that it assumes understanding and empathy on the part of employees because of who they are, rather than because of their training, ability and qualifications (Lewis, 2000: 88). This could impact negatively on employees and on their delivery of services (ibid.).

4.4 Best Value

The introduction of Best Value as a framework for service procurement and delivery, replacing CCT, enables local authorities to take a strategic overview of service delivery which can include consideration of issues of equity as well as efficiency, effectiveness and economy. However, it is too early to say with any certainty whether the Best Value regime will have a positive impact on social inclusion, community empowerment and equality in service delivery. But the Best Value regime has also been used to introduce standard performance measurements across a range of local authority activities. This includes measurements of achievement in numbers of women in senior positions, numbers of ethnic minority employees and adoption of and level reached within the CRE Standard. In addition to these corporate health measurements, there are user satisfaction surveys. These surveys have been designed to provide data on how satisfied local people are with the range of services provided by their local authority. These surveys also gather socio-economic characteristics and can thus provide some indication of how satisfied or dissatisfied people are by gender, ethnicity and disability. Breakdowns of data can also be done for age and occupation.

The Audit Commission (2002a) has just published a report, *Equality and Diversity: learning from audit, inspection and research*, which examines Best Value Performance Indicators (BVPIs) for the information they offer on how well local authorities in England and Wales are doing in providing equality of service to disabled people, ethnic minorities and women. The information detailed below is based on this report.

4.4.1 EMPLOYMENT (BVPIS 11, 16 AND 17)[4]

The number of local authority, senior management posts filled by women is measured by BVPI 11. On average, 22 per cent of senior management posts in local authorities in England were filled by women (ibid., 41). The Audit Commission report notes that 'These average figures mask large variations between similar councils'. For example, the average for London Boroughs is 30 per cent of senior management posts filled by women, but this ranges between a minimum of 0 per cent and a maximum of 51 per cent (ibid.).

BVPI 16 measures the percentage of staff in local authorities who have self-defined as disabled. On average, just two per cent of local authority employees in England were disabled. As with BVPI 11 (women in senior management posts), there is wide variation between similar councils (ibid., 43).

The proportion of local authority staff who are from an ethnic minority is measured by BVPI 17. The average for local authorities in England is just over 3 per cent of the total workforce (ibid., 44). While there are large differences between councils, this can be partly accounted for by the different geographical pattern of settlement for ethnic minority populations (ONS, 1996; Lakey, 1997). Further analyses by the Audit Commission show that the majority of local authorities do not have an ethnic staff profile which is representative of the local minority ethnic population in percentage terms (AC 2002a: 46). It should be noted, however, that the Audit Commission's analyses only compare all 'non-white' ethnic minorities combined with a homogeneous 'white' group[5].

---

4   BVPI 11: The percentage of senior management posts filled by women, where senior management posts refers to the top three tiers of management in the authority.
    BVPI 16: The percentage of local authority employees declaring that they meet the Disability Discrimination Act (1995) disability definition compared with the percentage of economically active disabled people in the area.
    BVPI 17: The percentage of local authority employees from minority ethnic communities compared with the percentage from the economically active minority ethnic community population in the authority area (DTLR, 2000).
5   The ethnic categories used in the user satisfaction surveys followed the 2001 Census ethnic category question. Broad headings (white, mixed, Black/Black British, Asian/Asian British, Chinese) were used under which further specification was required.

4.4.2 CRE STANDARD (BVPI 2)

By 1999/2000, fifty per cent of local authorities in England had adopted the CRE Standard; however, in 2000/1 over forty per cent had not achieved level 1 of the Standard as measured by BVPI 2 (ibid., 17)[6]. This suggests that there is still some way to go before local authorities can confidently assert that they address race equality in a holistic way across the range of services and functions. The Equality Standard (introduced in 2002/3) has now replaced the CRE Standard. It allows local authorities to self-assess their level of achievement in delivering equality for women and disabled people, as well as ethnic minorities; part of the rationale behind it is to enable local authorities to mainstream equalities (EO, 2002). Its framework permits the introduction of other areas relevant to equality such as age, sexuality and faith (ibid.). It remains to be seen whether adoption and implementation of this Standard is higher; however, as it covers a broader range of groups, it may be seen as relevant by local authorities which rejected the CRE Standard, particularly those who did so because they had low numbers of ethnic minority populations.

4.4.3 USER SATISFACTION SURVEYS

When Best Value Performance Indicators from the user satisfaction surveys are examined, some broad conclusions can be reached. Women tend to be more satisfied with the overall service provided by their local authority and across the range of services measured by BVPIs than men; similarly disabled people are more satisfied than those who are not disabled. White British people are more satisfied with the overall service provided by their authority than are respondents from any other ethnic group (as measured by BVPI 3: see Table 4.1 below for breakdown). This pattern is broadly replicated across other user satisfaction indicators: white British people are the most satisfied, with ethnic minority groups registering much higher levels of dissatisfaction.

4.4.4 AUDIT COMMISSION INSPECTIONS

The Audit Commission's report on equality and diversity additionally provides an analysis of 27 inspection reports from which conclusions about equality and diversity might be drawn (ibid., 47–70). This analysis suggests that there are reasons for concern regarding differences between equalities policies *per se* and outcome indicators; in other words, local authorities are poor at achieving outcomes related to equality policies (ibid., 52). This could be because the production of policy is itself seen as an achievement; lack of leadership on or ownership of equality policies by elected members; uneven implementation of equality policies across departments within local authorities; lack of conceptualisation of what implementation might mean (ibid.).

4.5 BVPI: Secondary Analysis of BVPI 3[7]

The Best Value surveys carried out by local authorities in England include surveys of user satisfaction. These surveys cover a range of local authority services, and it would be beyond

---

6   Level 1 of the CRE Standard (the lowest level) specifies that there must be a corporate written policy on racial equality and a policy for each service delivery area. The policies should have been subject to public consultation and agreed by members.

7   This section is based on data from the 2000/2001 Best Value user satisfaction surveys.

the scope of this small review to examine findings in detail. The Audit Commission's (2002a) publication *Equality and Diversity: learning from inspection audit and research* provides breakdowns of BVPI data by gender, ethnicity (broken down into a black/white dichotomy) and disability relating to equality and diversity.

Instead, this section will focus on indicator 3 (BVPI3), which measures respondents' satisfaction with the overall service provided by their local authority. Examining this particular BVPI measure indicates that it may be interesting to examine other indicators from the user satisfaction surveys in more depth. However, a measure of overall satisfaction may mask dissatisfaction with specific services or, indeed, dissatisfaction with specific services may depress the overall level of satisfaction. Thus it is only a broad indicator of satisfaction among service users.

A general observation is that women and disabled people tend to express higher levels of satisfaction than do men or non-disabled people. In contrast, ethnic minority groups generally tend to express lower levels of satisfaction and higher levels of dissatisfaction than do white British people. There needs to be some caution about interpreting results by ethnic group as numbers in some groups are very low and thus satisfaction ratings recorded may be idiosyncratic rather than representative. Cross tabulations (see tables in Annex A) heighten this likelihood. Overall, the samples of all ethnic minority groups are not representative of overall population size for ethnic groups in England (see Table 1.1, Annex A).

4.5.1 AGE

Generally, satisfaction increases with age, so that those over retirement age are the most satisfied by age (see Table 4.1, below). Those aged under 18 record higher rates of satisfaction than the next two age groups (18–24 and 25–34). This may be because of smaller numbers in this age group, or it may reflect better services for those aged under 18.

Table 4.1 Satisfaction with Overall Service Provided by Local Authority (BVPI3) by age, percentages				
Age Group	Satisfied	Neither	Dissatisfied	% of Total
Under 18	60.3	25.8	13.9	1.3
18–24	58.1	28.0	13.9	6.6
25–34	59.1	28.0	12.9	13.7
35–44	61.9	25.7	12.5	17.5
45–54	62.9	23.9	13.1	18.2
55–64	67.3	21.0	11.6	16.5
65–74	72.1	18.3	9.7	15.1
75+	75.7	16.9	7.4	9.9
Not stated	57.4	25.5	17.2	1.1
Total	65.2	23.1	11.8	100

4.5.2 DISABILITY

Respondents to the user satisfaction surveys who were registered disabled generally had higher rates of satisfaction with local authority services overall compared to people who did not describe themselves as disabled (see Table 4.2, below). This may reflect better services for disabled people, or lower expectations among disabled people. The pattern for increasing satisfaction with age (excluding under 18s) is repeated for registered disabled respondents. However, disaggregation by age group shows that respondents who are not registered disabled have higher satisfaction ratings across all age groups (except under 18s) than do registered disabled respondents (Table 2.1, Annex A).

Table 4.2 Satisfaction with Overall Service Provided by Local Authority (BVPI3) by disability, percentages				
Disability	Satisfied	Neither	Dissatisfied	% of Total
Registered disabled	66.2	20.9	12.9	24.1
Not registered	64.5	23.9	11.5	74.5
Don't know	61.9	21.6	16.5	0.1
Not stated	66.4	20.9	12.6	1.2
Total	65.0	23.1	11.9	100

4.5.3 GENDER

Overall, women express more satisfaction with their local authority than do men responding to the user satisfaction survey (see Table 4.3, below). British and Irish women are the most satisfied across the ethnic groups; in general, however, women from all ethnic groups tend to express more satisfaction than do their male peers.

Women of all ages tend to be more satisfied compared to their male peers. Generally, satisfaction increases with age for both men and women (Table 2.2, Annex A). Older men, from 65 onwards, tend to have satisfaction ratings similar to those for older women. This may possibly reflect: generational differences – older people in general are more likely to express satisfaction; better services for older people; increased use or knowledge of services by men following on from retirement. In particular, it should be noted that the changes over time which lead to higher satisfaction among men and women could be due to less people saying they are neither satisfied nor dissatisfied – although as the data is based on one survey, this is speculation.

Disabled women have similar satisfaction ratings to disabled men (67.1 per cent satisfied compared to 65.2) (Table 2.3, Annex A). This contrasts with women and men who are not registered disabled, where there is a clearer difference in satisfaction ratings: 66.7 per cent of women who are not registered disabled are satisfied with the overall service provided by their local authority, compared to 61.9 per cent of men who are not registered disabled.

Table 4.3 Satisfaction with Overall Service Provided by Local Authority (BVPI3) by gender, percentages				
Gender	Satisfied	Neither	Dissatisfied	% of Total
Men	62.8	23.9	13.2	45.5
Women	66.8	22.4	10.7	54.0
Not stated	64.1	22.4	13.4	0.5
Total	65.0	23.1	11.9	100

4.5.4 ETHNICITY

Respondents from ethnic minority groups are, generally, more likely than white British people to say they are dissatisfied with the overall service offered by their local authority. The exceptions to this are white Irish respondents and Chinese respondents. White Irish respondents express nearly the same level of satisfaction as do white British respondents; however, higher levels of dissatisfaction than white British people are also recorded for white Irish people (11.5 compared to 14.6 per cent, Table 4.4, below). Chinese people record relatively low levels of satisfaction and dissatisfaction. However, caution needs to be applied to any finding for the individual ethnic minority groups because of the tiny numbers concerned; any findings may not be robust at this level. The Audit Commission (2002a) combined ethnic minority groups to create a black/white dichotomous comparison, finding that on a range of measures the 'black' group had higher levels of dissatisfaction than did the 'white' group. In the same report, it was noted that at ethnic group level, there was a complex set of different findings (ibid.).

The general gender pattern of women expressing more satisfaction than men holds to some extent across the ethnic groups in the survey (Table 2.4, Annex A). White British women express the highest levels of satisfaction of any of the ethnic groups when examined by gender. Caribbean women and women from the 'other Black' category are the most likely women to express dissatisfaction (22.6 and 24.3 per cent respectively). The highest levels of dissatisfaction are among the Pakistani and Bangladeshi ethnic groups (21.4 and 21.0 per cent, respectively), with Pakistani and Bangladeshi men registering very high levels of dissatisfaction (56.1 and 59.0 per cent respectively).

Table 4.4 Satisfaction with Overall Service Provided by Local Authority (BVPI3) by ethnic group, percentages

Ethnic group	Satisfied	Neither	Dissatisfied	% of Total
White	65.4	23.0	11.6	95.8
British	65.6	23.0	11.5	93.6
Irish	65.1	20.2	14.6	0.9
Other white	54.1	28.2	17.7	1.4
Mixed	59.4	26.3	14.3	0.4
White & Caribbean	59.1	26.5	14.4	0.1
White & African	60.8	21.9	17.3	0.0
White & Asian	62.7	25.1	12.2	0.1
Other mixed	54.5	30.1	15.4	0.1
Asian	57.0	25.2	17.8	1.6
Indian	55.2	27.9	16.9	0.7
Pakistani	56.7	21.9	21.4	0.4
Bangladeshi	58.0	21.6	20.4	0.1
Other Asian	61.0	24.4	14.6	0.3
Black	55.8	23.8	20.4	0.7
Caribbean	53.8	24.8	21.4	0.4
African	61.4	20.6	18.0	0.2
Other Black	48.4	28.9	22.7	0.1
Chinese	53.6	35.5	10.9	0.2
Other ethnic background	58.6	25.7	15.7	0.2
Not stated	58.0	23.4	18.6	1.2
Total	65.0	23.1	11.8	100

There is a general pattern across the ethnic groups of satisfaction increasing with age (Table 2.5, Annex A). The quite high satisfaction among the under 18 age group may be affected by the low numbers within this category. However, along with the small sample sizes for ethnic groups (except white British), it should also be recalled that ethnic minority populations have a different age structure from the white British population. Generational differences may be different (with older members of ethnic minorities being more likely to have migrated to Britain) from those in the white British group. This may be reflected in the higher satisfaction ratings for older ethnic respondents. The higher satisfaction ratings among older ethnic respondents also follows the general pattern of increasing satisfaction with age.

In general, disabled respondents from ethnic minority groups express higher levels of dissatisfaction than do white British disabled respondents (Table 2.6, Annex A). This reverses the general trend of disabled respondents expressing higher levels of satisfaction (Table 4.2, above), but again these frequencies are based on very small numbers of respondents so may not be indicative of actual opinion.

4.5.5 EMPLOYMENT

Respondents who are retired are the most satisfied by occupation at time of survey (see Table 4.5, below); this may in part reflect the more general trend of increasing satisfaction with increasing age. Respondents who describe themselves as permanently sick/disabled expressed the most dissatisfaction.

Across all types of economic activity, women express more satisfaction than men, although there is very little difference in satisfaction between retired men and retired women (Table 2.7, Annex A). In general, satisfaction increases with age regardless of economic activity, reflecting the finding that older men and women have similar satisfaction ratings in BVPI 3 (see also Table 2.8, Annex A). Those who work full-time in the home also express more satisfaction – and this is one of the few instances when men express higher levels of satisfaction than do women, although older women in this category record higher satisfaction levels than do men, which may reflect the higher likelihood that older men do not classify themselves as working in the home. Lowest satisfaction ratings are from self-employed men, closely followed by men on a government support scheme and men in full-time education.

In terms of ethnic group, the lowest overall satisfaction ratings are recorded for Chinese people who are permanently sick/disabled (Table 2.9, Annex A). This contrasts with satisfaction ratings by ethnicity alone, where Chinese people were most likely to say they were neither satisfied nor dissatisfied (Table 4.4, above). The higher satisfaction ratings for retired people do not hold true across all the different ethnic groups. However, some combinations of ethnicity by employment activity have very small numbers, leading in some instances to 100 per cent ratings, so these results are probably not reflective of the wider populations of these ethnic groups.

Disabled people in full-time education are the least satisfied among disabled respondents when examined by economic activity type (Table 2.10, Annex A). This may reflect the slower pace of implementation of the Disability Discrimination Act in the higher education sector and/or problems concerning support for disabled people in education. Among disabled people, the most satisfied by economic activity are those who are retired, reflecting age difference already observed.

Table 4.5 Satisfaction with Overall Service Provided by Local Authority (BVPI3) by occupation at time of survey, percentages

Occupation	Satisfied	Neither	Dissatisfied	% of Total
Full-time employment	60.3	26.6	13.1	35.0
Part-time employment	66.4	23.1	10.5	11.4
Self employed	60.0	26.2	13.8	7.7
Government scheme	62.1	23.8	14.1	0.5
Full-time education	59.9	27.9	12.2	2.4
Unemployed	63.6	22.2	14.1	2.4
Permanently sick/disabled	64.7	20.0	15.4	4.7
Retired	72.0	18.6	9.5	23.4
Working in the home	69.6	20.5	9.9	10.4
Other	65.7	21.8	12.5	1.2
Not stated	67.9	19.6	12.7	0.8
Total	67.6	19.7	12.7	100

4.5.6 AUTHORITY TYPE

When examined by authority type, London Borough councils achieve the lowest overall satisfaction ratings for BVPI 3. This holds true across the different characteristics examined here. Interestingly, it also holds true for satisfaction among ethnic groups (see Table 4.6). Sample sizes for ethnic minority populations in London Boroughs were larger and thus this finding is perhaps more reliable than when examining satisfaction ratings for local authorities as a whole (in which sample ethnic minorities are under-represented). However, actual numbers are still small so these frequencies may not be reliable and should be treated with caution, as with the other tables for ethnic minority respondents. In part, this more proportionate sampling in London Boroughs reflects patterns of settlement; other individual authorities may have secured comparatively higher numbers of ethnic minority respondents but this may be masked within the authority type group into which they fall, with other similar authorities by type having smaller samples of ethnic minorities in their survey returns.

Table 4.6 **Satisfaction with Overall Service Provided by Local Authority (BVPI3) by ethnic group, London Borough Councils only, percentages**				
Ethnic group	Satisfied	Neither	Dissatisfied	% of Total
White	55.4	24.5	20.1	78.1
British	56.1	24.3	19.6	69.1
Irish	55.6	22.0	22.4	2.8
Other white	47.1	28.1	24.8	6.2
Mixed	52.9	27.6	19.5	1.3
White & Caribbean	52.4	27.4	20.2	0.3
White & African	55.8	15.4	28.8	0.2
White & Asian	54.7	29.9	15.4	0.4
Other mixed	51.0	29.9	19.1	0.5
Asian	48.9	28.7	12.4	7.9
Indian	45.2	31.3	23.5	4.2
Pakistani	53.1	25.4	21.5	1.3
Bangladeshi	52.4	23.6	0.9	0.9
Other Asian	53.2	27.4	19.3	1.6
Black	50.4	25.8	23.9	7.1
Caribbean	47.4	27.8	24.8	3.9
African	55.7	22.4	21.9	2.7
Other Black	43.7	29.1	27.2	0.5
Chinese	45.6	38.0	16.3	0.9
Other ethnic background	50.8	24.0	25.1	0.6
Not stated	50.2	22.3	27.5	4.1
Total	54.2	25.0	20.8	100

Chapter Summary

As a major provider of services, either directly or indirectly through sub-contracting, local government has an important role to play in the promotion and delivery of equality and diversity. The introduction of Best Value in 2000 (replacing Compulsory Competitive Tendering) enables local authorities to give consideration to wider issues than cost in service delivery. The Best Value regime includes the measurement of service delivery by local authorities. Data from the Best Value user satisfaction surveys shows that overall ethnic minority service users tend to express more dissatisfaction than do white British service users. Women and disabled people tend to express more satisfaction than do men and people who are not registered disabled, respectively.

The business case for diversity emphasises a match between employees and service users: thus the diversity of service users in reflected in those delivering the services. However, this approach assumes that diversity in invested in employees characteristics, rather than being effected through training and awareness.

CHAPTER 5
Conclusions

5.1 Conclusions

It is important not to see the three themes examined in this review (representation, participation and leadership, employment, and service delivery) as separate from each other. Policies, including those on equal opportunities or equality, are developed by officers and approved by elected members. Thus both officers and members are responsible for delivering and ensuring delivery of equality in the range of local authority activities. However, policies may remain only paper policies and result in little or no action. Indeed, even where there is a commitment to equality and equal treatment, too often this is interpreted within the local government sector as meaning that everyone should be treated the same. This approach wrongly assumes that equality means ignoring difference, rather than accepting and accommodating difference. Thus women chief executives are expected to conform to traditional male patterns of working; gender-blind and race-blind approaches which ignore or deny difference may, however, result in inequalities.

While the three strands do overlap and can be mutually reinforcing, this does not necessarily imply a positive or negative relationship among them. There is no evidence to suggest, for example, that the election of women or ethnic minority councillors necessarily means equalities are improved or introduced into employment and/or service areas within local government. This may be because of the difficulties faced by women and ethnic minority councillors themselves: racism, sexism, lack of promotion to positions of power from which they could influence such matters. It should also be noted that it is not necessarily the case that a councillor who is from a particular group will identify with and understand the needs and circumstances of that group. Older women and ethnic minority councillors, for example, may not be fully apprised of or appreciate the particular concerns and needs of young women or young people from ethnic minorities.

However, it must be recognised that local authorities have been trailblazers in the field of equalities and that there are many examples of good and best practice to be found in this sector. Local authorities are important sources of employment for women and ethnic minority people, for example. This partly reflects the positive impact of equal opportunities policies, race units, women's units and equalities units within local authorities and particularly their influence on recruitment practices. It also reflects the initial concentration on employment for equal opportunities policies. Other factors, such as flexible working policies can be important for employees who have family and/or caring responsibilities. However, good practice in recruitment has not always been followed through to ensure equal opportunities in promotion and development. There is also some evidence that there are some problems of sexism and racism for staff within local authorities, coming from both fellow staff and members. These problems cut across the three themes examined in this literature review.

There is a public sector case to be made for equality and diversity which is analogous to the business case outlined by Rutherford and Ollearernshaw (2002), but different from it. As with the business case, this encompasses issues of fairness in employment practices (recruitment, retention, development and training), having a good reputation, access to a wider client or customer base and the avoidance of expensive litigation as a consequence of discrimination. However, for the public sector, there are also issues of equality of access and representation which are not apparent in the business case. Of course, equality in access and representation does not imply equal access or equal/proportionate representation. Rather, it means that access and representation must be appropriate and effective. Such an approach suggests that equality of access to services means that, where appropriate, different needs should be addressed and that substantive representation is important but not reliant on actual representation. The public sector case for equality, like the business case, requires leadership, in this case from chief officers and elected members. The evidence reviewed here raises the question of whether chief officers and elected members are equipped or willing to provide this leadership. The public sector case for equality is a case which recognises that all stakeholders should have an investment in the delivery of equality and diversity. For example, better employment practices within a local authority may reduce both staff turnover and expensive tribunal cases, thus making savings which can be applied to other aspects of authority business.

The implementation of the Employment and Race Directives, which include new protections with regard to religion, belief and sexuality, as well as relating to gender, race and disability may have implications for how local authorities manage equality and diversity as an employer. They will add to the existing package of legislation (Race Relations (Amendment) Act, Disability Discrimination Act, Sex Discrimination Act, Equal Pay Act) already in effect. The literature surveyed here highlights problems and issues of concern relating to women, ethnic minority groups and, to a lesser extent, young people. The gaps in the literature on equality and diversity in local government relate to class, disabled people, sexual orientation, religious belief and faith, and nomadic groups. It remains to be seen how local authorities in England will meet the challenge of implementing the new directives (as legislated for), particularly with regard to groups which have perhaps not traditionally been incorporated into equality and diversity policies and practices. The track record of local government in this field means that expectations of local government's delivery in this new area is high[1].

The user satisfaction surveys undertaken as part of the Best Value regime provide local authorities with information on how well they are doing generally in terms of service delivery and customer satisfaction, enabling local authorities to identify problem areas and areas where they are perceived to be doing well. Additionally, this information can be used to identify levels of satisfaction and dissatisfaction among different sub-groups of the population. As these surveys will be repeated, this will in the future provide indicative data on how well local authorities are doing in delivering and improving services to the satisfaction of different sub-groups of service users. Overall, however, it is at present unclear what current practice, in terms of delivering equality and diversity, might be in the local government sector in England[2]. It should also be borne in mind, however, that the delivery of equality and diversity by local authorities is a currently rapidly changing area which local government has to grapple with and on which it is expected to deliver, in part because of its historic role in promoting equal opportunities, but also because it is a major deliverer of services to the public.

1   Speech by Barbara Roche, at the *Ending Discrimination on the Grounds of RELIGION, BELIEF AND SEXUALITY – local government leading the way* conference, 21 November 2002.

2   No baseline of practice across local authorities in England has yet been established, although a research project has been commissioned by the Local and Regional Government Research Unit in the Office of the Deputy Prime Minister, which should go some way to remedy this.

Chapter Summary

It is important not to see the three themes in this review (representation, participation and leadership; employment; service delivery) as separate from each other. Local authorities have been leaders in the promotion of equalities, and there are many examples of good and best practice to be found.

There is a public sector case to be made for equality and diversity which is analogous to, but distinct from, the business case. As with the business case, this encompasses issues of fairness in employment practices (recruitment, retention, development and training), having a good reputation, access to a wider client of customer base and the avoidance of expensive litigation as a consequence of discrimination. However, the public sector case also implies equality of access to services and that different needs of different groups should be addressed in service delivery, regardless of employee profile.

BIBLIOGRAPHY

1996 "Making the break through" *Recreation*, April 1996, 36–7.

Adolino, J.R. 1998a *Ethnic Minorities, Electoral Politics and Political Integration in Britain* Pinter: London, Washington.

Adolino, J.R. 1998b "Integration within the British political parties: perceptions of ethnic minority councillors" in S. Saggar (ed) *Race and British Electoral Politics* UCL Press: London.

Amin, K. and Richardson, R. 1998 "The public policy agenda: campaigning and politics for a multi-ethnic good society", chapter 11 in S. Saggar (ed) *Race and British Electoral Politics*, UCL Press: London.

Anderson, E. 1999 "What is the point of equality?" *Ethics* 109, 287–337.

Anderson, I., Percy-Smith, J. and Dowson, L. 2001 "The role of research in 'modern' local government", *Local Government Studies*, 27(3), 59–78.

Association of Metropolitan Authorities and the Metropolitan Authorities Recruitment Agency 1993 *Women and Local Government: a directory of local government initiatives* AMA London.

Atkinson, S. and Boyle, J. 1996 "Young people and local authorities: what can we do to make them more interested - should we bother?" *Local Government Policy Making* 23(3), 22–29.

Audit Commission 2002a *Equality and Diversity: learning from audit, inspection and research* AC: London.

Audit Commission 2002b *Recruitment and Retention: strategic challenge* AC: London.

Audit Commission 1995 *Talk Back: local authority communication with citizens* HMSO: London.

Back, L. and Solomos, J. 1992 "Who Represents Us? Racialized politics and candidate selection" *Research Papers* No 3, Dept. of Politics and Sociology, Birkbeck: London.

Bailey, D. and Jones, A. 2001 "Evaluating Equalities" *Local Government Studies* 27(2), 1–18.

Ball, W. and Solomos, J. 1990 *Race and Local Politics* Macmillan: London.

Barnes, C. 2002 "Introduction: disability, policy and politics" *Policy and Politics*: special issue on Disability Politics: representation and voices in the policy process 30(3), 311–318.

Barnes, M. 2002 "Bringing difference into deliberation? Disabled people, survivors and local governance" *Policy and Politics*: special issue on Disability Politics: representation and voices in the policy process 30(3), 319–332.

Beck, U. 1992 *The Risk Society: towards a new modernity*, Sage: London.

Birch, D. and Purdy, D. 2001 *Work-Life Balance: a survey of local authorities* DTLR: London.

Bochel, C. and Bochel, H.M. 2000 *The Careers of Councillors: gender, party and politics* Ashgate: Aldershot.

Bourne, J. 2001 "The life and times of institutional racism" *Race and Class* 43(2), 7–22.

Bovaird, T. and Löffler, E. 2002 "Moving from excellence models of local service delivery to benchmarking 'good local governance'" *International Review of Administrative Sciences* 68(1), 9–24.

Bretherton, C. 2001 "Gender mainstreaming and EU enlargement: swimming against the tide?" *Journal of European Public Policy* 8(1), 60–81.

Briggs, J. 2000 "'What's in it for women?' The motivations, expectations and experiences of female local councillors in Montreal, Canada and Hull, England" *Local Government Studies* 26(4), 71–84.

Bristow, S. 1980 "Women councillors: an explanation of the under-representation of women in local government" *Local Government Studies* 6(3), 73–90.

Bromley, C., Curtice, J. and Seyd, B. 2001 "Political engagement, trust and constitutional reform", chapter 9 in *British Social Attitudes, 18th report: Public policy, social ties* Sage and National Centre for Social Research: London.

Brown, A.R., Jones, A. and Mackay, F. 1999 *The 'Representativeness' of Councillors* Joseph Rowntree Foundation: York.

Brownill, S. and Thomas, H. 1998 "Ethnic minorities and British urban policy: a discussion of the trends in governance and democratic theory" *Local Governance* 24(1), 43–55.

Bruegel, C. and Kean, H. 1995 "The moment of municipal feminism: gender and class in 1980s local government" *Critical Social Policy* 15(2), 147–169.

Busby, N. and MacLeod, C. 2002 "Maintaining a balance: the retention of women MPs in Scotland" *Parliamentary Affairs* 55, 30–42.

Cabinet Office 2002 *Government to carry out biggest review of equality in 25 years*, CAB 053/02.

Canavon, M. and Smith, P. 2001 *Representing the People: democracy and diversity* LGA: London.

Carmines, E.G., Huckfeldt, R. and McCurley, C. 1995 "Mobilization, counter-mobilization and the politics of race" *Political Geography* 14(6), 601–19.

Charlesworth, J. 2002 "The new duty to promote racial equality", *Briefing* March 2002, 14.

Children and Young People's Unit 2002 *Young People and Politics: a report on the YVote/YNot? Project* CYPU: London.

Chivite-Matthews, N.I. and Teal, J. 2001 1998 *British Social Attitudes Survey: secondary analysis of the local government module*, DTLR: http://www.local.dtlr.gov.uk/research/surv1998/index.htm

Clarke, J. and Speeden, S. 2000 *Measuring Up? A report of a study of the adoption and implementation of Racial Equality Means Quality, the Commission for Racial Equality's Standard for Local Government* CRE: London.

Collier, R. 1998 *Managing Equality in Service Delivery*, Open University Press: Milton Keynes.

Collis, C., Green, A. and Mallier, T. 2000 "Older female workers in Britain and its regions" *Local Economy* 15(1), 45–58.

Commission for Racial Equality 1998 *Racial Equality Means Quality* (revised edition) CRE: London.

Commission on the Future of Multi-Ethnic Britain 2000 *The Future of Multi-Ethnic Britain: the Parekh report* Profile Books: London.

Committee of the Regions 1999 *The Proportion of Women Members of Regional and Local Parliaments and Assemblies in the EU* COR (CdR 405/99 D/Ho/ym): Brussels.

Committee of the Regions 2001 *Voter Turnout at Regional and Local Elections in the European Union 1990–2001* COR (I-3/2001): Brussels.

Copus, C. 2001 "Citizen participation in local government: the influence of the political party group" *Local Governance* 27(3), 151–163.

Courtenay, G., Finch, S., Rao, N. and Young, K. 1998 *The Impact of Releasing People for Council Duties* DETR: London.

Cross, M. with Brar, H. and McLeod, M. 1991 "Racial Equality and the Local State: an evaluation of of policy implementation in the London Borough of Brent" *Monographs in Ethnic Relations* No1 ESRC & Centre for Research in Ethnic Relations: Coventry.

Daly, N. 1997 "Job-size scheme will provide legal defence: traditional female jobs to be boosted in new local government scheme" *Personnel Today* 27 March 1997.

Davidson, M.J. 1997 *The Black and Ethnic Minority Woman Manager: cracking the concrete ceiling* PCP: London.

Dibben, P. and Bartlett, D. 2001 "Local government and service users: empowerment through user-led innovation?" *Local Government Studies*, 27(3), 43–58.

Disability Rights Commission 2002 *Disability Briefing, May 2002*, DRC: London.

Dromey, J. 1998 "Best value and best employment" *Local Economy* August 1998, 98–101.

DETR 1998 *Modern Local Government: in touch with the people*, DETR: London.

DTI 2002 *Equality and Diversity: the way ahead*, DTI: London.

DTLR 2001 *Strong Local Leadership – Quality Public Services*, CM5237. SO: London.

Dunne, G.A., Prendergast, S. and Telford, D. 2002 "Young, gay, homeless and invisible: a growing population?" *Culture, Health and Sexuality*, 4(1), 103–115.

Edwards, J. and McKie, L. 1993/4 "The European Economic Community – a vehicle for promoting equal opportunities in Britain?" *Critical Social Policy* 13(3), 51–65.

Employers' Organization 2002 *Census of Local Authority Councillors: comparisons, 1997–2000* EO: London.

Employers' Organization 2002b "Employee jobs in local government, June 2001" *Local Government Employment Digest* May 2002.

Employers' Organization 2002c 'Research and Intelligence: frequently asked question', http://www.lg-employers.gov.uk/research/faq.htm

Escott, K. and Whitfield, D. 1995 *The Gender Impact of CCT in Local Government* EOC Research Discussion Series: Manchester.

Fagan, C. 1996 "Gendered time schedules: paid work in Great Britain" *Social Politics* Spring, 72–106.

Fagan, C., O'Reilly, J. and Rubery, J. 1998 "Part-time work: challenging the 'breadwinner' gender contract", chapter 13 in J. Jensen, J. Laufer and M. Maraumi (eds) *The Gendering of Inequalities: women, men and work* Ashgate: Aldershot.

Fair, J. 1997 "Ethnic minority managers face career discrimination" *Municipal Journal* 42, 7.

Fair, J. 1999 "Racism goes public" *Personnel Today* 15 April 1999, 33–4.

Fitzgerald, M. 1984 *Political Parties and Black People: participation, representation and exploitation* Runnymede Trust: London.

Foley, K. 2002 "Local economies and the impact of the privatization of public services" *Local Economy* 17(1), 2–7.

Foley, M. and McVicar, A. 2001 "The gender implications of workplace flexibility on local government leisure sector employees in Scotland" *Leisure Studies* 68, 113–124.

Foley, P. and Martin, S. 2000 "A new deal for the community? Public participation in regeneration and local service delivery" *Policy and Politics* 28(4), 479–91.

Fox, P. and Broussine, M. 2001 *Room At The Top? A study of women chief executives in local government in England and Wales* Bristol Business School, UoWE: Bristol.

Froud, H. 2000 "Old prejudices still blight women managers" *Guardian*, Society supplement 9 November 2000.

Game, C. and Leach, S. 1993 "Councillors and local democracy" *Research Link* No. 3, 12–13.

Gardiner, C. 2001 "Informing policy making: new approaches to analysing the 2001 census" *Local Government Studies*, 27(4), 71–88.

Geddes, A. 2001 "Explaining ethnic minority representation: contemporary trends and the shadow of the past" *British Elections and Parties Review* 11, 119–135.

Geddes, M. 2002 "Involving young people in local democracy in the UK - tensions in New Labour's 'Third Way'" *Lien Social et Politiques* 48 (draft copy provided by author).

Geddes, M. 2001 "What about the workers? Best value, employment and work in local public services" *Policy and Politics* 29(4), 497–508.

Geddes, M. and Newman, I. 2002 "How local authorities can make a difference: benchmarking best practice" *Local Authorities and Social Inclusion Network* Report 10.

Geddes, M. and Root, A. 2000 "Social exclusion – new language, new challenges for local authorities" *Public Money and Management*, April–June, 55–60.

Geddes, M. and Rust, M. 1999 "Involving young people in local government and local democracy: findings from the evaluation of three local initiatives" *Warwick University Local Authority Research Consortium Research Paper* No 29: Coventry.

Giddy, P. 2000 *A Woman's Place is in the Chamber: first thoughts on attracting women into local politics* LGA first thoughts series: London.

Gill, B. 2000 *Losing Out Locally: women and local government* Fawcett: London.

Guardian Research Department 2002 "Muslim Britain: the statistics" *The Guardian* 17 June 2002.

Hall, K. and Horton, L. 2002 *Public Service Delivery: women's experiences and views: qualitative research findings* Women and Equality Unit: London.

Harris, L. 2000 "Issues of fairness in recruitment processes: a case study of local government practice" *Local Government Studies* 26(1), 31–46.

Hawes, D. and Perez, B. 1995 *The Gypsy and the State: the ethnic cleansing of British society* SAUS Bristol.

Heath, A. and MacMahon, D. 1997 "Education and occupational attainment: the impact of ethnic origins" on V. Karn (ed) *Education, Employment and Housing among Ethnic Minorities in Britain*, HMSO: London.

Hibbet, A. 2002 *Gender Briefing* Women and Equality Unit, May 2002.

Hickman, M.J., Morgan, S. and Walter, B. 2001 *Second-Generation Irish People in Britain: a demographic, socio-economic and health profile*, University of North London: London.

Hickman, M.J. and Morgan, S. 1997 *The Irish in Lewisham*, Lewisham Irish Community Centre: London.

Hickman, M.J. and Walter, B. 1997 *Discrimination and the Irish Community in Britain: a report of research*, CRE: London.

Higginbottom, K. 2002 "Democratic deficit" *People Management* 27 June 2002, 16–17.

Hills, J. 1982 "Women local councillors - a reply to Bristow" *Local Government Studies* January.

Hinds, K. and Jarvis, L. 2000 "The gender gap", chapter 5 in R. Jowell, J. Curtice, A. Park, K. Thomson, L. Jarvis, C. Bromley, and N. Stratford (eds) *British Social Attitudes, the 17th Report: focusing on diversity* Sage/National Centre for Social Research: London.

Hogwood, B.W. 1998? "Towards a new stucture of public employment in Britain?" *Policy and Politics* 26(3), 321–341.

Holly, L. 1998 "The glass ceiling in local government: a case study" *Local Government Studies* 24(1), 60–73.

Howes, M. 2002 "Women in UNISON - in Cardiff" *Briefing* March 2002, 15.

IDeA and EO 2001 *2000 Exit Survey of Local Authority Councillors*, IDeA/EO: London.

IDeA and EO 1999 *1998 Survey of Newly Elected Councillors in England*, IDeA/EO: London.

IPPR 2001 "Involving young people in decision making: a survey of local authorities" *Research Briefing* No 10 IPPR/LGA: London.

Johnston, M. and Jowell, R. 2001 "How robust is British civil society?" chapter 8 in A. Park, J. Curtice, K. Thomson, L. Jarvis and C. Bromely (eds) *British Social Attitudes, the 18th Report: public policy, social ties*, Sage/National Centre for Social Research: London.

Karn, V. (ed) 1997 *Ethnicity in the 1991 Census* vol 4 "Employment, education and housing among the ethnic minority populations of Britain" SO: London.

Kean, D. 1996 "Moving on up: women are heavily under-represented in senior posts in local government" *Municipal Journal* 39, 20–21.

Keeton, K.B. 1996 "Characteristics of successful women managers and professionals in local government: a national survey" *Women in Management Review* 11(3), 27–34.

Kessler, I., Purcell, J. and Shapiro, J.C. 2000 "Employment relations in local government: strategic choice and the case of Brent" *Personnel Review* 29(2), 162–87.

Kettle, J. 1998 "Local initiatives for working women: feminism, economics or both?" *Local Government Studies* 24(4), 64–76.

Kimberlee, R.H. 2002 "Why don't British young people vote at general elections?" *Journal of Youth Studies* 5(1), 85–98.

Klages, H. and Löffler, E. 2002 "Giving staff of local authorities a voice: a checklist of success factors for staff surveys" *Local Governance* 28(1), 13–22.

Kopfeld, C.W. and Sprague, J. 2002 "Race, space and turnout" *Political Geography* 21(2), 175–94.

Lakey, J. 1997 "Neighbourhoods and housing" chapter 6 in T. Modood et al *Ethnic Minorities in Britain: diversity and disadvantage, The Fourth National Survey of Ethnic Minorities* PSI: London.

Lanquetin, M.T. 1998 "Equality at work: what difference does legislation make?", chapter 17 in J. Jensen, J. Laufer and M. Maraumi (eds) *The Gendering of Inequalities: women, men and work* Ashgate: Aldershot.

Latta, M. 2000 "Side-streaming gender? The potential and pitfalls of the European ideology on mainstreaming and gender issues" *Transfer* 6(2), 290–320.

LGMB 1998 *Evening the Odds: research into management development for black and other minority ethnic managers* LGMB: London.

Lewis, G. 2000 *'Race', Gender and Social Welfare: encounters in a postcolonial society*. Polity: Cambridge.

Local Government Association 2001 "Involving young people in decision-making: a survey of local authorities" *Research Briefing* No 10, LGA: London.

Local Government Association 2001 *Representing the People: democracy and diversity* LGA: London.

Local Government Association 2000 *Local Leadership, Local Progress: a survey of local authorities on political management and probity* LGA: London.

Local Government Association 2002 *Faith and Community: a good practice guide for local authorities* LGA: London.

Lovenduski, J. "Gender politics: a breakthrough for women?" *Parliamentary Affairs* 50(4), 708–719.

Lowndes, V., Pratchett, L. and Stoker, G. 2001a "Trends in public participation: part 1 – local government perpectives" *Public Administration* 79(1), 205–222.

Lowndes, V., Pratchett, L. and Stoker, G. 2001b "Trends in public participation: part 2 – citizens' perspectives" *Public Administration* 79(2), 445–55.

Maddock, S. 2002 "Modernization requires transformational skills: the need for a gender-balanced workforce" *Women in Management Review* 17(1), 12–17.

Maddock, S. 1995 "Rhetoric and reality: the business case for equality and why it continues to be resisted" *Women in Mangement Review* 10.

Martin, S. 2001 "Reevaluating public service improvement: the early impacts of the Best Value regime" *Policy and Politics* 29(4) 467–50.

Mason, A. 2001 "Equality of opportunity, old and new" *Ethics* 111, 760–781.

Mason, D. 1990 "Competing conceptions of 'fairness' and the formulation and implementation of equal opportunities policies", chapter 3 in W. Ball and J. Solomos (eds) *Race and Local Politics* Macmillan: London.

May, J. 1996 "Globalization and the politics of of place: place and identity in an inner London neighbourhood" *Transactions Institute of British Geographers* 21(1), 194–215.

McLeod, M., Owen, D. and Khamis, C. 2001 *Black and Minority Ethnic Voluntary and Community Organisations: their role and future development in England and Wales*, PSI: London.

McRae, S. 1990 "Women at the top: the case of British national politics" *Parliamentary Affairs* 43(3), 341–7.

Meadowcroft, J. 2001 "Community politics, representation and the limits of deliberative democracy" *Local Government Studies* 27(3), 25–42.

Modood, T. 2000 "La place des musulmans dans le multiculturalisme laïc en Grande-Bertagne" *Social Compass* 47(1), 41–55.

Modood, T., Berthoud, R., Lakey, J. Nazroo, J., Smith, P., Virdee, P. and Beishon, S. 1997 *Ethnic Minorities in Britain: diversity and disadvantage, The Fourth National Survey of Ethnic Minorities* PSI: London.

Modood, T. 1997 "Employment" chapter 4 in T. Modood et al *Ethnic Minorities in Britain: diversity and disadvantage. The Fourth National Survey of Ethnic Minorities* PSI: London.

Molloy, D., White, C. and Hosfield, N. 2002 *Understanding Youth Participation in Local Government: a qualitative study* DTLR: London.

Morgan, P. and Allington, N. 2002 "Has the public sector retained its 'model employer' status?" *Public Money and Management* Jan-Mar, 35–42.

MORI 2000 *The People's Panel: ethnic booster sample summary report* MORI: London.

MORI 2002 *The Voice of Britain: Britain beyond rhetoric - headline findings from a research study conducted for the Commission for Racial Equality* CRE: London.

Muddiman, D., Durrani, S., Dutch, M., Linley, R., Pateman, J. and Vincent, J. 2000 *Open to All? The public library and social exclusion*. Volume 2: Survey, case studies and methods Resource (The Council for Museums, Archives and Libraries): Boston Spa.

Nagel, C. 2002 "Constructing difference and sameness: the politics of assimilation in London's Arab communities" *Ethnic and Racial Studies* 25(2), 258–287.

Nagel, C. 2001 "Hidden minorities and the politics of 'race': the case of British Arab activists in London" *Journal of Ethnic and Migration Studies* 27(3), 381–400.

Nanton, P. 1998 "Community politics and the problem of partnership: ethnic minority participation in urban regeneration", chapter 10 in S. Saggar (ed) *Race and British Electoral Politics* UCL Press: London.

National Statistics 2002 *Ethnicity: Labour Market, Bangladeshis' unemployment highest*, briefing on NS webpages: http://www.statistics.gov.uk/CCI/nugget.asp?ID=271&Pos=2&ColRank=2&Rank=1000

Nixon, J. 1998 "The role of black and Asian MPs at Westminster", chapter 9 in S. Saggar (ed) *Race and British Electoral Politics* UCL Press: London.

Noon, M. and Hoque, K. 2001 "Ethnic minorities and equal treatment: the impact of gender, equal opportunities policies and trade unions" *National Institute Economic Review* April 2001, No176, 105–115.

Office for Public Management 2001 *Making a Difference: women in public appointments: research findings for the Department for Transport, Local Government and the Regions* OPM: London.

ONS 2000 *Social Inequalities* (2000 edition) SO: London.

ONS 1995 *Social Focus on Women* HMSO: London.

ONS 1996 *Social Focus on Ethnic Minorities* HMSO: London.

Osborne, S.P. and McLaughlin, K. 2002 "Trends and issues in the implementation of local 'voluntary sector compacts' in England" *Public Money and Management* January-March, 55–63.

Ouseley, H. 1990 "Resisting institutional change", chapter 8 W. Ball and J. Solomos (eds) *Race and Local Politics* Macmillan: London.

Owen, D. 1995 "Irish-born people in Great Britain: settlement patterns and socio-economic circumstances" *1991 Census Statistical Paper* 9 CRER: Coventry.

Palmer, S. 2000 *One Year On: a review of local authority responses to the LGA, EO and IDeA's initial guidance on the Stephen Lawrence Inquiry* LGA, EO and IdeA: London.

Park, A. 2000 "The generation game", chapter 1 in R. Jowell, J. Curtice, A. Park, K. Thomson, L. Jarvis, C. Bromley, and N. Stratford (eds) *British Social Attitudes, the 17th Report: focusing on diversity* Sage/National Centre for Social Research: London.

Parker, D. 1995 *Through Different Eyes: the cultural identities of young Chinese people in Britain*, Avebury: Aldershot.

Parker, S. 2002 "Power struggle", *Guardian* Society supplement, 12 June 2002, 12.

Perfect, D. 1995 *The Gender Impact of CCT in Local Government*, pamphlet EOC: Manchester.

Perrons, D. 2000 "Flexible working and equal opportunities in the United Kingdom: a case study from retail", *Environment and Planning* A 32, 1719–1734.

Perrott, S. 2002 "Gender, professionals and management in the public sector" *Public Money and Management* Jan-Mar 2002.

Pitts, J. and Hope, T. 1997 "The local politics of inclusion: the state and community safety" *Social Policy and Administration*, 31(5), 37–58.

PIU 2002 *Ethnic Minorities and Labour Markets: interim analysis report* PIU: London.

PIU 2000 *Reaching Out: the role of central government at regional and local level* SO: London.

Prasad, R. 2002 "Tough justice" *The Guardian*, 10 June 2002.

Pratchett, L. 2000 *Renewing Local Democracy? The modernisation agenda in British local government* Frank Cass: London, Portland.

Quirk, B. 1999 "Blame, shame and leadership", *Public Finance*, 3–9 December 1999, 16–18.

Rallings, C. and Thraser, M. 1999 "An audit of local democracy in Britain: the evidence from local elections" *Parliamentary Affairs*, 52(1), 58–76.

Rallings, C., Thrasher, M., Downe, J., Ridge, M., Jansen, M., Preston, I. And Lowry, M. 2000 *Turnout at Local Government Elections: influences on levels of voter registration and eletoral participation* DETR: London.

Randall, S. 1991 "Local government and equal opportunities in the 1990s" *Critical Social Policy* 11(1), 38–58.

Rao, N. 2000a *A Survey of Women Councillors in Local Government: preliminary findings*.

Rao, N. 2000b *Political Representativeness in British Local Government: a survey of non-working councillors* Nuffield Foundation website.

Rao, N. 1999 "Representing the people? Testing assumptions about local government reform" *Public Administration* 77(2), 257–71.

Rao, N. 1998 "Representation in local politics: a reconsideration and some new evidence" *Political Studies* 46, 19–35.

RCU 2002 *Review of Area-Based Initiatives* ODPM: London.

Roker, D., Player and Coleman, J. 1999 "Young People's voluntary and campaigning activities as sources of political education" *Oxford Review of Education* 25(1/2), 185–98.

Rutherford, S. and Ollerearnshaw, S. 2002 *The Business of Diversity: how organisations in the public and private sectors are integrating equality and diversity to enhance business performance* Schneider-Ross: Andover.

Saggar, S. (ed) 1998 *Race and British Electoral Politics* UCL Press: London.

Saggar, S. and Geddes, A. 2000 "Negative and positive racialisation: re-examining ethnic minority political representation in the UK" *Journal of Ethnic and Migration Studies* 26(1), 25–44.

Scott, R. and Morris, G. 2002 *Polls Apart 3* Scope with DRC: London.

Scott-Hill, M 2002 "Policy, politics and the silencing of 'voice'" *Policy and Politics*: special issue on Disability Politics: representation and voices in the policy process 30(3), 397–410.

Shaw, A. 2002 "Why might young British Muslims support the Taliban?" *Anthropology Today* 18(1), 5–8.

Simmons-Lewis, S. 2002 "Best in the business", *Local Government Chronicle*, 30.08.2002 LGC London.

Simpson, S. 1997 "Demography and ethnicity: case studies from Bradford" *Journal of Ethnic and Migration Studies* 23(1), 89–107.

Singh, G. 2001 "Winning the race challenge" *Employment Matters* 25, 4–5.

Solomos, J. and Back, L. 1995 *Race, Politics and Social Change* Routledge: London, NY.

Solomos, J. and Singh, G. 1990 "Racial equality, housing and the local state", chapter 6 in W. Ball and J. Solomos (eds) *Race and Local Politics* Macmillan: London.

Spencer, S. 2000 "Making race equality count: measuring progress towards race equality" *New Economy* 7(1), 35–40.

Sperling, L. 1998 "Public Services, quangos and women: a concern for local government" *Public Administration* 76, 471–87.

Tate, C. 1998 "Ethnic lessons" *Nursing Management* 5(1), 5.

Taylor, F. 2001 "Connecting young people to local government" *Local Governance* 27(3), 121–31.

Taylor, M., Craig, G. and Wilkinson, M. 2002 "Co-option or empowerment? The changing relationship between the state and the voluntary and community sectors" *Local Governance* 28(1), 1–11.

Thomas, H. and Lo Piccolo, F. 2000 "Best value, planning and race equality" *Planning Practice and Research* 15 (1/2), 79–94.

Tomlins, R. 1999 *Housing Experiences of Minority Ethnic Communities in Britain: an academic literature review and annotated bibliography* CRER: Coventry.

Unison 2001 *Making a Difference Under Pressure: Unison members delivering local services* Unison: London.

Unison 2002a "Winning Equal Pay: equal pay developments in the UK" *Unison Briefing* No 1, April 2002.

Unison 2002b *Equal Pay and Best Value: getting equal* £ Unison London.

Wade, H., Lawton, A. and Stevenson, M. 2001 *Hear By Right: setting standards for the active involvement of young people in democracy*, LGA/NYC: London.

Walzer, B. 2001 *Outsiders Inside* Routledge: London.

Webb, J. 2001 "Gender, work and transitions in the local state", *Work, Employment and Society*, 15(4), 825–44.

Welch, S. 1990 "Multi-member districts and the representation of women: evidence from Britain and the United States" *Journal of Politics* 52(2), 391–412.

Welch, S. and Studlar, D.T. 1990 "Multi-member districts and the representation of women: evidence from Britain and the United States" *Journal of Politics* 52(2), 391–412.

West Midlands Forum 1998 *Racial Equality: common standards for council contracts – spotlighting and implementing a common standard for assessing service providers*, WMF: Birmingham.

Wilford, R., Miller, R., Bell, Y. and Donoghue, F. 1993 "In their own voices: women councillors in Northern Ireland" *Public Administration* 71(Autumn), 341–355.

Willow, C. 1999 *Hear! Hear! Promoting children and young people's democratic participation in local government* LGIU London.

Wren, J. 2002 "The Equality Standard for local government - back to the beginning", *Briefing* March 2002, 12–13.

Young, K. 1990 "Approaches to policy development in the field of equal opportunities" in W. Ball and J. Solomos (eds) *Race and Local Politics* Macmillan: London.

Young, K. 1997 "Beyond policy and politics: contingencies of employment equity" *Policy and Politics* 25(4).

Yule, J. 2000 "Women councillors and committee recruitment" *Local Government Studies* 26(3), 31–54

ANNEX A

1 Breakdowns by socio-economic characteristics

Table 1.1 Comparison of percentage of respondents by ethnic group in BVPI Survey (England) with 2001/2 Annual Local Area Labour Force Survey (UK) and 2001 Census (England)

Ethnic Group	BVPI survey	2001/2 LFS	2001 Census
White British	93.4	92.4	86.99
White Irish	0.9		1.27
Other white background	1.4		2.66
Mixed White & Caribbean	0.1	0.8	0.47
Mixed White & African	0.0		0.16
Mixed White & Asian	0.1		0.37
Other mixed background	0.1		0.31
Indian	0.7	1.7	2.09
Pakistani	0.4	1.3	1.44
Bangladeshi	0.1	0.5	0.56
Other Asian background	0.3	0.4	0.48
Caribbean	0.4	1.0	1.14
African	0.2	0.9	0.97
Other Black background	0.1	0.1	0.19
Chinese	0.2	0.3	0.45
Other ethnic background	0.2	0.6	0.44
Not stated	1.3	0.2	

Table 1.2 Comparison of percentage of respondents by gender in BVPI survey with 2001 Census for England

Gender	BVPI survey	2001 Census
Men	45.2	48.7
Women	54.2	51.3
Not stated	0.6	–

Table 1.3 Comparison of percentages of respondents by age in BVPI survey with 2001 Census for England

Age group	BVPI survey	2001 Census
Under 18	1.3	2.5*
18–24	6.5	8.4
25–34	13.5	14.4
35–44	17.3	14.9
45–54	18.0	13.2
55–64	16.5	10.5
65–74	15.3	8.3
75+	10.3	7.5
Not stated	1.3	–

* Percentage of 16 and 17 year olds in 2001 Census; all under 18 constitutes 22.7%.

2 Crosstabulations for BVPI 3

Table 2.1 Satisfaction with Overall Service Provided by Local Authority (BVPI3) age by whether registered disabled, percentages

		Age group				
Whether disabled		**< 18**	**18–24**	**25–34**	**35–44**	**45–54**
Registered disabled	Satisfied	62.5	53.8	56.4	57.9	60.5
	Neither	23.0	26.1	27.1	25.8	23.1
	Dissatisfied	14.6	20.1	16.5	16.3	16.4
Not registered	Satisfied	59.5	58.5	59.4	62.3	63.5
	Neither	26.8	28.2	28.1	25.7	24.2
	Dissatisfied	13.7	13.2	12.5	12.0	12.3
Don't know	Satisfied	–	33.3	83.3	68.6	64.7
	Neither	–	66.7	16.7	20.0	17.6
	Dissatisfied	–	–	–	11.4	17.6
Not stated	Satisfied	71.2	61.5	59.5	63.4	62.0
	Neither	16.9	19.9	27.2	23.3	22.1
	Dissatisfied	11.9	18.6	13.3	13.2	15.8

		Age group				
		55–64	**65–74**	**75+**	**Not**	
Whether disabled					**stated**	**Total**
Registered disabled	Satisfied	65.9	70.3	73.9	58.2	66.3
	Neither	20.5	18.6	17.9	24.5	20.9
	Dissatisfied	13.6	11.1	8.2	17.4	12.8
Not registered	Satisfied	68.0	73.3	77.7	56.1	64.7
	Neither	21.3	18.1	15.8	26.5	23.9
	Dissatisfied	10.8	8.7	6.5	17.4	11.4
Don't know	Satisfied	73.5	65.9	62.2	59.3	61.9
	Neither	14.7	25.0	28.9	21.1	21.5
	Dissatisfied	11.8	9.1	8.9	19.7	16.5
Not stated	Satisfied	66.7	70.8	77.6	59.2	67.0
	Neither	20.8	18.3	15.8	24.9	20.7
	Dissatisfied	12.5	10.9	6.6	15.8	12.3

Table 2.2 Satisfaction with Overall Service Provided by Local Authority (BVPI3) gender by age, percentages

Age group		Men	Women	Not stated	Total
		Gender			
Under 18	Satisfied	57.7	62.5	75.0	60.3
	Neither	26.5	25.2	25.0	25.8
	Dissatisfied	15.8	12.4	–	13.9
18–24	Satisfied	56.2	59.6	58.3	58.1
	Neither	29.0	27.3	29.2	28.0
	Dissatisfied	14.8	13.2	12.5	13.9
25–34	Satisfied	54.4	62.3	61.8	59.1
	Neither	30.1	26.5	26.5	28.0
	Dissatisfied	15.4	11.2	11.8	12.9
35–44	Satisfied	57.2	65.3	61.8	61.8
	Neither	27.9	24.0	23.6	25.7
	Dissatisfied	14.9	10.6	14.5	12.5
45–54	Satisfied	59.7	65.7	62.1	62.9
	Neither	25.3	22.7	22.7	23.9
	Dissatisfied	15.0	11.5	15.2	13.1
55–64	Satisfied	65.3	69.3	70.0	67.3
	Neither	22.1	20.1	22.0	21.0
	Dissatisfied	12.7	10.6	8.0	11.6
65–74	Satisfied	71.0	73.1	71.1	72.1
	Neither	18.6	17.9	17.8	18.3
	Dissatisfied	12.7	10.6	8.0	11.6
75+	Satisfied	76.3	75.1	79.5	75.7
	Neither	16.1	17.6	17.0	16.9
	Dissatisfied	7.5	7.3	3.4	7.4
Not stated	Satisfied	55.2	55.2	62.9	57.4
	Neither	25.0	27.4	22.9	25.4
	Dissatisfied	19.8	17.4	14.2	17.2

Table 2.3 Satisfaction with Overall Service Provided by Local Authority (BVPI3) gender by disability, percentages

Whether disabled		Men	Women	Not stated	Total
		Gender			
Registered disabled	Satisfied	65.2	67.1	67.3	66.2
	Neither	20.9	20.9	18.5	20.9
	Dissatisfied	13.9	11.9	14.2	12.9
Not registered disabled	Satisfied	61.9	66.7	65.3	64.6
	Neither	25.1	22.9	23.6	23.9
	Dissatisfied	13.0	10.3	11.2	11.5
Don't know	Satisfied	59.6	67.3	57.6	62.0
	Neither	27.3	16.6	22.6	21.6
	Dissatisfied	13.0	16.1	19.8	16.4
Not stated	Satisfied	64.7	68.7	63.5	66.4
	Neither	21.1	20.1	23.1	20.9
	Dissatisfied	14.2	11.2	13.4	12.6

Table 2.4 Satisfaction with Overall Service Provided by Local Authority (BVPI3) gender by ethnic group, percentages

Ethnic Group		Gender			
		Men	Women	Not stated	Total
White British	Satisfied	63.3	67.4	66.7	65.5
	Neither	23.9	22.3	21.4	23.0
	Dissatisfied	12.8	10.3	12.0	11.5
White Irish	Satisfied	62.8	66.9	64.7	65.1
	Neither	20.7	19.9	23.5	20.3
	Dissatisfied	16.5	13.1	11.8	14.6
Other white background	Satisfied	52.0	56.0	68.8	54.1
	Neither	28.4	28.2	6.3	28.2
	Dissatisfied	19.6	15.8	25.0	17.7
Mixed White & Caribbean	Satisfied	57.5	59.9	100 (3)	59.1
	Neither	26.8	26.6	–	26.5
	Dissatisfied	15.7	13.6	–	14.4
Mixed White & African	Satisfied	58.9	63.8	50.0	61.8
	Neither	23.3	20.6	–	21.5
	Dissatisfied	17.8	15.6	50.0	16.7
Mixed White & Asian	Satisfied	62.7	63.2	100 (2)	63.0
	Neither	23.2	26.7	–	24.8
	Dissatisfied	14.1	10.2	–	12.1
Other mixed background	Satisfied	55.8	54.1	100 (1)	54.9
	Neither	29.8	29.3	–	29.5
	Dissatisfied	14.4	16.6	–	15.6
Asian Indian	Satisfied	53.1	57.7	50.0	55.3
	Neither	29.0	26.5	50.0	27.8
	Dissatisfied	17.9	15.8	–	16.9
Asian Pakistani	Satisfied	56.1	56.9	80.0	56.5
	Neither	22.5	21.6	–	22.0
	Dissatisfied	21.4	21.5	20.0	21.4
Asian Bangladeshi	Satisfied	59.0	57.5	50.0	58.2
	Neither	20.0	23.1	25.0	21.6
	Dissatisfied	21.0	19.4	25.0	20.2
Other Asian background	Satisfied	61.3	59.9	100 (1)	60.6
	Neither	25.7	23.4	–	24.6
	Dissatisfied	12.9	16.7	–	14.8
Black Caribbean	Satisfied	56.7	51.5	66.7	53.8
	Neither	23.3	25.9	16.7	24.8
	Dissatisfied	20.0	22.6	16.7	21.5
Black African	Satisfied	64.7	58.3	50.0	61.3
	Neither	16.9	24.0	50.0	20.7
	Dissatisfied	18.4	17.7	–	18.0
Other Black background	Satisfied	47.2	48.6	–	48.0
	Neither	32.0	27.1	–	29.1
	Dissatisfied	20.8	24.3	–	22.8
Chinese	Satisfied	53.9	53.3	50.0	53.6
	Neither	36.4	34.6	50.0	35.6
	Dissatisfied	9.8	12.1	–	10.9
Other ethnic background	Satisfied	57.2	59.4	60.0	58.4
	Neither	26.4	24.8	20.0	25.5
	Dissatisfied	16.4	15.8	20.0	16.1
Not stated	Satisfied	56.5	59.6	56.0	58.0
	Neither	24.3	22.3	26.0	23.5
	Dissatisfied	19.2	18.1	18.0	18.6

Table 2.5 Satisfaction with Overall Service Provided by Local Authority (BVPI3) age by ethnic group, percentages

Ethnic Group		Age group				
		< 18	18–24	25–34	35–44	45–54
White British	Satisfied	60.4	58.6	59.7	62.4	63.3
	Neither	25.9	28.1	28.0	25.6	23.9
	Dissatisfied	13.7	13.2	12.2	12.0	12.8
White Irish	Satisfied	72.7	66.0	56.3	60.3	64.2
	Neither	15.9	19.8	29.7	23.3	19.1
	Dissatisfied	11.4	14.2	14.0	16.4	16.7
Other white background	Satisfied	60.4	55.2	48.6	51.1	51.2
	Neither	20.8	33.1	29.9	30.0	29.4
	Dissatisfied	18.8	11.6	21.5	18.9	19.4
Mixed White & Caribbean	Satisfied	50.0	48.9	60.6	58.7	61.0
	Neither	25.0	32.2	25.2	27.8	28.0
	Dissatisfied	25.0	18.9	14.2	13.5	11.0
Mixed White & African	Satisfied	–	64.3	66.1	55.0	63.6
	Neither	100 (2)	14.3	14.3	26.7	22.7
	Dissatisfied	–	21.4	19.6	18.3	13.6
Mixed White & Asian	Satisfied	75.0	57.8	54.4	59.0	69.9
	Neither	18.8	23.9	31.0	28.4	21.5
	Dissatisfied	6.3	18.3	14.6	12.7	8.6
Other mixed background	Satisfied	75.0	43.8	47.1	55.8	55.0
	Neither	25.0	38.0	33.3	33.7	25.0
	Dissatisfied	–	18.2	19.5	10.5	20.0
Asian Indian	Satisfied	52.0	49.8	56.8	51.0	57.4
	Neither	36.0	28.6	26.8	31.0	26.9
	Dissatisfied	12.0	21.6	16.4	18.0	15.7
Asian Pakistani	Satisfied	81.3	56.8	51.1	57.8	59.6
	Neither	18.8	19.8	25.2	18.8	20.8
	Dissatisfied	–	23.5	23.7	23.4	19.6
Asian Bangladeshi	Satisfied	70.0	54.5	56.9	67.0	58.7
	Neither	10.0	23.4	22.2	17.9	27.0
	Dissatisfied	20.0	22.1	21.0	15.1	14.3
Other Asian background	Satisfied	100 (8)	57.3	52.2	57.2	64.5
	Neither	–	25.6	28.5	25.3	23.3
	Dissatisfied	–	17.1	19.3	17.5	12.3
Black Caribbean	Satisfied	54.5	36.5	49.5	53.6	58.1
	Neither	9.1	33.3	26.1	27.4	22.8
	Dissatisfied	36.4	30.1	24.4	19.0	19.1
Black African	Satisfied	100 (4)	50.6	54.7	66.8	74.1
	Neither	–	31.0	21.2	17.1	12.2
	Dissatisfied	–	18.5	24.1	16.1	13.6
Other Black background	Satisfied	–	43.9	49.2	45.0	45.2
	Neither	–	33.3	29.2	25.0	38.1
	Dissatisfied	–	22.8	21.5	30.0	16.7
Chinese	Satisfied	50.0	58.2	42.5	58.8	48.0
	Neither	50.0	34.1	43.0	32.9	39.9
	Dissatisfied	–	7.7	14.5	8.2	12.1
Other ethnic background	Satisfied	33.3	40.8	56.6	60.1	54.6
	Neither	66.7	41.8	28.0	22.6	29.5
	Dissatisfied	–	17.3	15.4	17.3	15.8
Not stated	Satisfied	40.0	60.9	50.3	52.3	50.9
	Neither	40.0	18.5	29.5	25.2	25.9
	Dissatisfied	20.2	20.6	20.1	22.5	23.2

(Continued overleaf)

Table 2.5 **Satisfaction with Overall Service Provided by Local Authority (BVPI3) age by ethnic group, percentages (Cont.)**						
		Age group				
Ethnic Group		55–64	65–74	75+	Not stated	Total
White British	Satisfied	67.7	72.3	75.9	58.3	65.7
	Neither	20.9	18.2	16.8	25.3	23.0
	Dissatisfied	11.4	9.5	7.3	16.3	11.4
White Irish	Satisfied	66.1	70.5	76.5	66.7	65.3
	Neither	18.3	17.5	15.5	12.1	20.4
	Dissatisfied	15.7	11.9	8.0	21.2	14.3
Other white background	Satisfied	54.9	64.6	67.3	51.2	54.1
	Neither	27.1	23.5	20.8	27.9	28.3
	Dissatisfied	18.0	11.9	11.9	20.9	17.6
Mixed White & Caribbean	Satisfied	58.2	64.2	72.7	66.7	59.1
	Neither	29.1	18.9	18.2	11.1	26.5
	Dissatisfied	12.7	17.0	9.1	22.2	14.4
Mixed White & African	Satisfied	62.5	76.9	100 (3)	60.0	62.6
	Neither	25.0	23.1	–	–	20.7
	Dissatisfied	12.5	–	–	40.0	16.7
Mixed White & Asian	Satisfied	78.4	73.9	73.7	20.0	62.4
	Neither	17.6	21.7	10.5	60.0	25.4
	Dissatisfied	3.9	4.3	15.8	20.0	12.2
Other mixed background	Satisfied	75.0	69.4	77.8	75.0	54.8
	Neither	20.0	16.7	16.7	–	30.0
	Dissatisfied	5.0	13.9	5.6	25.0	15.1
Asian Indian	Satisfied	64.0	66.7	50.6	57.6	55.4
	Neither	24.1	19.2	36.5	30.3	27.8
	Dissatisfied	11.9	14.1	12.9	12.1	16.8
Asian Pakistani	Satisfied	66.5	51.0	72.7	55.6	56.4
	Neither	20.3	32.3	13.6	22.2	22.0
	Dissatisfied	13.3	16.7	13.6	22.2	21.6
Asian Bangladeshi	Satisfied	48.5	54.5	76.5	60.7	58.1
	Neither	24.2	24.2	17.6	10.7	21.7
	Dissatisfied	27.3	21.2	5.9	28.6	20.2
Other Asian background	Satisfied	58.8	68.8	72.1	–	61.0
	Neither	26.9	20.5	20.6	100 (1)	24.6
	Dissatisfied	14.3	10.8	7.3	–	14.4
Black Caribbean	Satisfied	60.0	68.2	65.0	37.5	54.0
	Neither	21.8	17.7	13.8	43.8	24.9
	Dissatisfied	18.2	14.1	21.3	18.8	21.1
Black African	Satisfied	68.8	65.7	70.6	50.0	61.7
	Neither	19.8	20.0	23.5	25.0	20.2
	Dissatisfied	11.5	14.3	5.9	20.5	18.1
Other Black background	Satisfied	62.1	69.2	44.4	–	48.1
	Neither	27.6	7.7	22.2	50.0	29.0
	Dissatisfied	10.3	23.1	33.3	50.0	22.9
	Dissatisfied	10.4	13.2	12.5	–	10.6
Other ethnic background	Satisfied	60.7	77.3	70.6	55.6	58.7
	Neither	21.4	17.3	11.8	22.2	26.0
	Dissatisfied	17.9	5.5	17.6	22.2	15.4
Not stated	Satisfied	57.9	67.7	74.0	51.5	58.4
	Neither	25.3	19.7	16.8	26.1	23.5
	Dissatisfied	16.8	12.7	9.2	22.5	18.1

Table 2.6 Satisfaction with Overall Service Provided by Local Authority (BVPI3) whether registered disabled by ethnicity

Ethnic group		Whether disabled				
		Registered disabled	Not registered	Don't know	Not stated	Total
White British	Satisfied	66.7	65.1	66.2	68.0	65.5
	Neither	20.8	23.8	20.1	20.1	23.0
	Dissatisfied	12.5	11.1	13.7	11.9	11.5
White Irish	Satisfied	66.4	64.7	25.0	64.9	65.1
	Neither	18.1	21.0	50.0	16.2	20.2
	Dissatisfied	15.6	14.3	25.0	18.9	14.7
Other white background	Satisfied	53.2	54.3	100 (2)	58.3	54.1
	Neither	26.4	28.5	–	25.0	28.1
	Dissatisfied	20.4	17.2	–	16.7	17.8
Mixed White & Caribbean	Satisfied	50.0	62.0	–	80.0	59.1
	Neither	34.7	23.5	–	20.0	26.3
	Dissatisfied	15.3	14.5	–	–	14.6
Mixed White & African	Satisfied	65.5	59.3	–	–	60.5
	Neither	20.0	22.7	–	100(1)	17.1
	Dissatisfied	14.5	18.0	–	–	17.1
Mixed White & Asian	Satisfied	70.5	60.5	–	100 (8)	62.8
	Neither	17.9	26.5	–	–	24.6
	Dissatisfied	11.6	13.0	–	–	12.6
Other mixed background	Satisfied	58.1	53.8	–	50.0	54.6
	Neither	26.9	30.5	–	50.0	29.9
	Dissatisfied	15.1	15.7	–	–	15.5
Asian Indian	Satisfied	56.9	54.9	–	37.5	55.2
	Neither	22.5	28.9	–	31.3	27.9
	Dissatisfied	20.6	16.2	–	31.3	16.9
Asian Pakistani	Satisfied	56.8	56.6	100(1)	80.0	56.8
	Neither	20.1	22.2	–	10.0	21.8
	Dissatisfied	23.1	21.1	–	10.0	21.4
Asian Bangladeshi	Satisfied	54.7	59.6	50.0	50.0	58.4
	Neither	22.7	20.8	–	41.7	21.5
	Dissatisfied	22.7	19.6	50.0	8.3	20.1
Other Asian background	Satisfied	59.4	58.7	–	–	58.8
	Neither	25.7	25.0	–	–	25.2
	Dissatisfied	14.9	16.3	–	–	16.0
Black Caribbean	Satisfied	55.1	53.3	–	61.9	53.8
	Neither	24.3	25.0	100(1)	28.6	24.9
	Dissatisfied	20.7	21.7	–	9.5	21.3
Black African	Satisfied	61.5	61.3	100(2)	85.7	61.6
	Neither	17.6	21.5	–	14.3	20.8
	Dissatisfied	20.9	17.2	–	–	17.6
Other Black background	Satisfied	43.2	52.3	–	66.7	50.2
	Neither	27.0	27.1	–	–	26.8
	Dissatisfied	29.7	20.6	–	33.3	23.0
Chinese	Satisfied	53.2	53.8	100(1)	66.7	53.9
	Neither	35.4	35.5	–	33.3	35.4
	Dissatisfied	11.4	10.7	–	–	10.7
Other ethnic background	Satisfied	63.6	57.1	–	100(4)	58.6
	Neither	16.6	28.0	–	–	25.6
	Dissatisfied	19.8	14.8	100(1)	–	15.8
Not stated	Satisfied	58.2	54.9	54.4	62.5	57.5
	Neither	22.1	24.7	25.1	23.0	23.8
	Dissatisfied	19.7	20.4	20.5	14.6	18.7

Table 2.7 **Satisfaction with Overall Service Provided by Local Authority (BVPI3)** gender by occupation at time of survey, percentages					
			Gender		
Occupation at time of survey		Men	Women	Not Stated	Totals
Full time employee	Satisfied	58.2	63.1	58.6	60.2
	Neither	27.4	25.5	26.3	26.6
	Dissatisfied	14.4	11.4	15.1	13.2
Part time employee	Satisfied	64.1	66.5	54.9	66.2
	Neither	23.2	23.2	33.0	23.2
	Dissatisfied	12.7	10.3	12.1	10.7
Self employed	Satisfied	58.1	62.6	60.6	59.8
	Neither	26.8	15.3	31.0	26.3
	Dissatisfied	15.1	12.0	8.5	14.0
Government scheme	Satisfied	58.3	64.5	85.7	61.9
	Neither	24.1	23.8	14.3	23.9
	Dissatisfied	17.6	11.8	–	14.2
Full time education	Satisfied	58.6	61.3	54.5	60.2
	Neither	28.1	27.3	27.3	27.7
	Dissatisfied	13.3	11.4	18.2	12.2
Unemployed	Satisfied	61.2	65.9	62.2	63.7
	Neither	22.7	21.2	21.6	22.1
	Dissatisfied	15.1	12.8	16.2	14.2
Permanently sick/disabled	Satisfied	64.2	65.0	63.9	64.6
	Neither	19.6	20.5	13.9	20.0
	Dissatisfied	16.3	14.4	22.2	15.4
Retired	Satisfied	71.6	71.9	73.8	71.8
	Neither	18.6	18.7	16.5	18.7
	Dissatisfied	9.8	9.4	9.7	9.6
Working in the home	Satisfied	71.8	69.3	63.6	69.5
	Neither	17.4	20.8	25.6	20.5
	Dissatisfied	10.8	9.9	10.7	10.0
Doing something else	Satisfied	63.1	66.6	64.5	65.3
	Neither	22.9	21.4	21.4	21.9
	Dissatisfied	14.0	12.1	14.1	12.8
Not stated	Satisfied	67.5	70.0	62.5	67.6
	Neither	18.6	18.8	23.2	19.7
	Dissatisfied	13.9	11.2	14.3	12.7

Table 2.8 Satisfaction with Overall Service Provided by Local Authority (BVPI3), age by occupation at time of survey, percentages

Occupation at time of survey		Age group				
		< 18	18–24	25–34	35–44	45–54
Full time employee	Satisfied	54.2	57.2	57.6	59.9	62.2
	Neither	29.1	29.0	29.6	27.0	24.5
	Dissatisfied	16.7	13.8	12.8	13.1	13.3
Part time employee	Satisfied	58.6	60.1	62.7	67.2	67.0
	Neither	27.1	27.2	25.7	23.3	22.5
	Dissatisfied	14.3	12.7	11.6	9.5	10.5
Self employed	Satisfied	54.7	58.1	55.6	56.6	59.5
	Neither	30.4	27.7	29.8	28.7	26.3
	Dissatisfied	14.9	14.2	14.7	14.7	14.3
Government scheme	Satisfied	67.5	53.9	58.9	60.5	66.7
	Neither	24.2	30.2	25.5	25.9	19.8
	Dissatisfied	8.2	15.9	15.6	13.6	13.5
Full time education	Satisfied	57.2	60.2	59.6	60.7	57.0
	Neither	30.2	28.2	26.0	28.0	27.4
	Dissatisfied	12.6	11.6	14.5	11.3	15.6
Unemployed	Satisfied	70.0	55.4	54.6	61.3	61.1
	Neither	19.0	26.5	26.1	23.8	23.3
	Dissatisfied	11.0	18.0	19.3	14.9	15.6
Permanently sick/disabled	Satisfied	55.8	48.6	54.8	60.2	62.0
	Neither	24.6	24.9	25.8	22.5	20.7
	Dissatisfied	19.6	26.5	19.4	17.3	17.3
Retired	Satisfied	68.4	56.8	66.8	66.9	63.4
	Neither	18.4	22.2	19.6	19.6	23.0
	Dissatisfied	13.2	21.1	13.6	13.5	13.6
Working in the home	Satisfied	63.2	57.6	64.5	67.7	66.0
	Neither	27.7	24.9	24.2	21.4	22.8
	Dissatisfied	9.2	17.4	11.3	10.9	11.2
Doing something else	Satisfied	68.3	57.0	58.2	58.0	65.0
	Neither	19.5	27.7	29.4	27.2	21.0
	Dissatisfied	12.2	15.3	12.4	14.8	14.0
Not stated	Satisfied	53.3	65.0	65.0	56.5	60.8
	Neither	30.0	22.5	23.1	32.3	23.5
	Dissatisfied	16.7	12.5	11.9	11.2	15.7

(Continued overleaf)

Table 2.8 Satisfaction with Overall Service Provided by Local Authority (BVPI3), age by occupation at time of survey, percentages (Cont.)

Occupation		55–64	65–74	75+	Not stated	Total
			Age group			
Full time employee	Satisfied	65.1	66.2	65.8	49.6	60.3
	Neither	22.8	22.6	21.5	29.1	26.6
	Dissatisfied	12.1	11.2	12.8	21.2	13.1
Part time employee	Satisfied	68.9	72.5	71.2	53.0	66.4
	Neither	20.8	17.4	19.2	29.2	23.1
	Dissatisfied	10.3	10.1	9.6	17.8	10.5
Self employed	Satisfied	64.0	68.8	71.6	52.1	60.0
	Neither	23.0	20.5	19.3	33.0	26.2
	Dissatisfied	13.0	10.7	9.1	14.9	13.8
Government scheme	Satisfied	67.9	72.9	77.8	43.8	62.1
	Neither	16.2	14.1	18.9	18.8	23.8
	Dissatisfied	15.9	12.9	3.3	37.5	14.1
Full time education	Satisfied	63.5	68.4	61.1	45.1	59.9
	Neither	20.3	21.1	25.0	33.8	27.9
	Dissatisfied	16.2	10.5	13.9	21.1	12.2
Unemployed	Satisfied	66.8	74.7	78.1	55.3	63.6
	Neither	20.9	16.9	14.8	26.6	22.2
	Dissatisfied	12.3	8.4	7.1	18.1	14.1
Permanently sick/disabled	Satisfied	67.0	70.7	72.2	57.1	64.7
	Neither	18.2	17.4	18.5	22.6	20.0
	Dissatisfied	14.8	12.0	9.3	20.3	15.4
Retired	Satisfied	69.0	71.8	75.5	64.4	72.0
	Neither	20.3	18.5	17.0	21.5	18.6
	Dissatisfied	10.6	9.7	7.5	14.1	9.5
Working in the home	Satisfied	70.8	74.3	78.3	56.5	69.6
	Neither	19.2	17.7	15.6	29.4	20.5
	Dissatisfied	10.0	8.0	6.0	14.2	9.9
Doing something else	Satisfied	68.0	72.5	76.1	60.4	65.7
	Neither	19.1	17.7	15.9	23.8	21.8
	Dissatisfied	12.9	9.8	8.0	15.8	12.5
Not stated	Satisfied	67.5	76.3	78.3	60.3	67.9
	Neither	19.1	13.9	14.6	22.5	19.6
	Dissatisfied	13.4	9.8	7.1	17.2	12.5

Table 2.9 Satisfaction with Overall Service Provided by Local Authority (BVPI3) occupation at time of survey by ethnic group, percentages

Ethnic group		Occupation at time of survey		
		Full time employee	Part time employee	Self employed
White British	Satisfied	60.7	66.6	60.2
	Neither	26.6	23.1	26.2
	Dissatisfied	12.7	10.3	13.6
White Irish	Satisfied	58.6	67.8	64.6
	Neither	24.7	19.0	18.6
	Dissatisfied	16.7	13.2	16.8
Other white background	Satisfied	49.4	55.4	51.3
	Neither	30.7	29.7	27.6
	Dissatisfied	19.9	14.9	21.1
Mixed White & Caribbean	Satisfied	58.2	57.7	53.1
	Neither	27.2	28.2	31.3
	Dissatisfied	14.7	14.1	15.6
Mixed White & African	Satisfied	57.5	75.9	46.7
	Neither	25.3	10.3	40.0
	Dissatisfied	17.2	13.8	13.3
Mixed White & Asian	Satisfied	59.3	64.1	70.7
	Neither	25.2	26.6	19.0
	Dissatisfied	15.4	9.4	10.3
Other mixed background	Satisfied	54.4	39.0	38.5
	Neither	23.8	46.3	42.3
	Dissatisfied	21.9	14.6	19.2
Asian Indian	Satisfied	51.1	60.7	51.0
	Neither	30.9	22.9	32.1
	Dissatisfied	18.0	16.4	16.9
Asian Pakistani	Satisfied	53.3	51.1	54.4
	Neither	21.8	30.4	30.4
	Dissatisfied	25.0	18.5	15.2
Asian Bangladeshi	Satisfied	55.7	53.8	55.9
	Neither	24.4	25.0	20.6
	Dissatisfied	19.8	21.2	23.5
Other Asian background	Satisfied	56.5	63.5	56.5
	Neither	25.7	18.9	29.6
	Dissatisfied	17.8	17.6	13.9
Black Caribbean	Satisfied	52.9	48.8	56.7
	Neither	27.5	22.8	26.8
	Dissatisfied	19.6	28.4	16.5
Black African	Satisfied	62.9	61.7	58.1
	Neither	17.8	18.8	22.6
	Dissatisfied	19.3	19.5	19.4
Other Black background	Satisfied	55.1	50.0	57.1
	Neither	24.6	38.5	14.3
	Dissatisfied	20.3	11.5	28.6
Chinese	Satisfied	53.1	47.7	54.7
	Neither	36.9	40.0	37.5
	Dissatisfied	10.0	12.3	7.8
Other ethnic background	Satisfied	59.3	53.5	50.0
	Neither	25.9	29.6	29.4
	Dissatisfied	14.8	16.9	20.6
Not stated	Satisfied	47.4	52.4	436
	Neither	26.8	24.8	23.5
	Dissatisfied	25.7	22.8	32.9
Totals	Satisfied	60.2	66.2	59.8
	Neither	26.6	23.2	26.3
	Dissatisfied	13.1	10.7	13.9

Table 2.9 **Satisfaction with Overall Service Provided by Local Authority (BVPI3)** occupation at time of survey by ethnic group, percentages (*Cont.*)				
		Occupation at time of survey		
Ethnic group		Government Scheme	Full time education	Unemployed
White British	Satisfied	63.2	61.2	64.5
	Neither	23.6	27.4	22.1
	Dissatisfied	13.1	11.4	13.5
White Irish	Satisfied	57.1	75.0	70.7
	Neither	23.8	20.5	18.8
	Dissatisfied	19.0	4.5	10.5
Other white background	Satisfied	47.5	56.7	46.3
	Neither	22.5	31.4	25.9
	Dissatisfied	30.0	11.9	27.8
Mixed White & Caribbean	Satisfied	57.1	39.4	66.7
	Neither	14.3	45.5	25.9
	Dissatisfied	28.6	15.2	7.4
Mixed White & African	Satisfied	71.4	60.0	33.3
	Neither	–	20.0	25.0
	Dissatisfied	28.6	20.0	41.7
Mixed White & Asian	Satisfied	42.9	56.9	60.7
	Neither	57.1	31.0	21.4
	Dissatisfied	–	12.1	17.9
Other mixed background	Satisfied	–	41.7	77.8
	Neither	100 (3)	53.4	–
	Dissatisfied	–	5.2	22.2
Asian Indian	Satisfied	48.7	47.3	65.9
	Neither	25.6	30.8	23.4
	Dissatisfied	25.6	21.9	10.8
Asian Pakistani	Satisfied	61.9	62.8	56.3
	Neither	9.5	15.7	17.8
	Dissatisfied	28.6	21.5	25.9
Asian Bangladeshi	Satisfied	54.5	59.6	62.7
	Neither	27.3	17.3	15.7
	Dissatisfied	18.2	23.1	21.6
Other Asian background	Satisfied	100 (1)	64.0	59.3
	Neither	–	31.5	23.7
	Dissatisfied	–	4.5	16.9
Black Caribbean	Satisfied	40.0	48.6	52.6
	Neither	35.0	19.3	27.5
	Dissatisfied	25.0	32.1	19.9
Black African	Satisfied	57.9	51.3	60.6
	Neither	26.3	27.9	23.4
	Dissatisfied	15.8	20.8	16.0
Other Black background	Satisfied	–	25.0	37.5
	Neither	25.0	60.7	37.5
	Dissatisfied	75.0	14.3	25.0
Chinese	Satisfied	100 (4)	53.0	37.9
	Neither	–	37.3	44.8
	Dissatisfied	–	9.7	17.2
Other ethnic background	Satisfied	58.3	41.3	71.4
	Neither	33.3	44.0	20.0
	Dissatisfied	8.3	14.7	8.6
Not stated	Satisfied	61.1	54.1	52.9
	Neither	16.7	21.6	25.9
	Dissatisfied	22.2	24.3	21.2
Totals	Satisfied	62.1	60.1	63.8
	Neither	23.7	27.7	22.2
	Dissatisfied	14.2	12.2	14.0

Table 2.9 Satisfaction with Overall Service Provided by Local Authority (BVPI3) occupation at time of survey by ethnic group, percentages (*Cont.*)

Ethnic group		Occupation at time of survey		
		Permanently sick/disabled	Retired	Working in the home
White British	Satisfied	65.0	72.1	70.1
	Neither	20.0	18.5	20.3
	Dissatisfied	15.0	9.4	9.6
White Irish	Satisfied	63.6	70.0	72.2
	Neither	17.0	17.1	16.3
	Dissatisfied	19.4	12.9	11.5
Other white background	Satisfied	52.7	62.3	58.6
	Neither	22.0	25.3	28.6
	Dissatisfied	25.4	12.4	12.8
Mixed White & Caribbean	Satisfied	59.1	71.2	63.4
	Neither	27.3	19.7	19.7
	Dissatisfied	13.6	9.1	16.9
Mixed White & African	Satisfied	86.7	71.4	56.5
	Neither	–	21.4	20.7
	Dissatisfied	13.3	7.1	13.8
Mixed White & Asian	Satisfied	70.0	78.1	54.8
	Neither	13.3	17.2	32.3
	Dissatisfied	16.7	4.7	12.9
Other mixed background	Satisfied	58.6	75.4	56.8
	Neither	20.7	17.5	25.0
	Dissatisfied	20.7	7.0	18.2
Asian Indian	Satisfied	58.7	60.0	67.7
	Neither	20.0	27.7	19.7
	Dissatisfied	21.3	12.3	12.6
Asian Pakistani	Satisfied	62.6	57.3	59.0
	Neither	19.1	25.5	22.6
	Dissatisfied	18.3	17.3	18.5
Asian Bangladeshi	Satisfied	61.5	50.0	64.3
	Neither	30.8	26.8	16.7
	Dissatisfied	7.7	23.2	19.0
Other Asian background	Satisfied	50.0	68.1	59.8
	Neither	27.9	24.7	20.5
	Dissatisfied	22.1	7.1	19.6
Black Caribbean	Satisfied	52.6	65.1	51.6
	Neither	22.6	19.3	26.1
	Dissatisfied	24.8	15.6	22.3
Black African	Satisfied	67.3	68.6	64.6
	Neither	14.5	21.6	20.7
	Dissatisfied	18.2	9.8	14.6
Other Black background	Satisfied	40.0	61.1	51.9
	Neither	20.0	27.8	29.6
	Dissatisfied	40.0	11.1	18.5
Chinese	Satisfied	16.7	62.2	56.5
	Neither	66.7	28.4	25.9
	Dissatisfied	16.7	9.5	17.6
Other ethnic background	Satisfied	43.9	74.1	59.0
	Neither	24.4	14.8	26.0
	Dissatisfied	31.7	11.1	15.0
Not stated	Satisfied	54.3	63.7	59.9
	Neither	19.9	21.8	22.4
	Dissatisfied	25.8	14.5	17.8
Totals	Satisfied	64.6	71.8	69.6
	Neither	20.0	18.6	20.5
	Dissatisfied	15.4	9.5	10.0

Table 2.9 Satisfaction with Overall Service Provided by Local Authority (BVPI3) occupation at time of survey by ethnic group, percentages (*Cont.*)

Ethnic group		Occupation at time of survey	
		Something else	Not stated
White British	Satisfied	66.1	69.8
	Neither	21.9	18.5
	Dissatisfied	12.0	11.7
White Irish	Satisfied	70.9	66.7
	Neither	14.5	25.0
	Dissatisfied	14.5	8.3
Other white background	Satisfied	60.8	56.8
	Neither	21.6	21.6
	Dissatisfied	17.6	21.6
Mixed White & Caribbean	Satisfied	25.0	33.3
	Neither	25.0	33.3
	Dissatisfied	25.0	33.3
Mixed White & African	Satisfied	50.0	–
	Neither	–	100 (2)
	Dissatisfied	50.0	–
Mixed White & Asian	Satisfied	42.9	100 (4)
	Neither	57.1	–
	Dissatisfied	–	–
Other mixed background	Satisfied	66.7	66.7
	Neither	33.3	33.3
	Dissatisfied	–	–
Asian Indian	Satisfied	60.0	90.0
	Neither	26.7	10.0
	Dissatisfied	13.3	–
Asian Pakistani	Satisfied	58.3	71.4
	Neither	19.4	21.4
	Dissatisfied	22.2	7.1
Asian Bangladeshi	Satisfied	52.9	50.0
	Neither	11.8	31.3
	Dissatisfied	35.3	18.8
Other Asian background	Satisfied	60.0	100 (1)
	Neither	20.0	–
	Dissatisfied	20.0	–
Black Caribbean	Satisfied	50.0	58.3
	Neither	22.2	16.7
	Dissatisfied	27.8	25.0
Black African	Satisfied	77.8	54.5
	Neither	11.1	36.4
	Dissatisfied	11.1	9.1
Other Black background	Satisfied	75.0	–
	Neither	–	–
	Dissatisfied	25.0	100 (2)
Chinese	Satisfied	75.0	40.0
	Neither	25.0	40.0
	Dissatisfied	–	20.0
Other ethnic background	Satisfied	55.0	66.7
	Neither	20.0	–
	Dissatisfied	25.0	33.3
Not stated	Satisfied	62.2	61.2
	Neither	22.2	23.0
	Dissatisfied	15.6	15.8
Totals	Satisfied	65.6	67.6
	Neither	21.8	19.7
	Dissatisfied	12.6	12.8

Table 2.10	Satisfaction with Overall Service Provided by Local Authority (BVPI3) whether registered disabled by occupation at time of survey, percentages

		Whether registered disabled				
Occupation		Registered disabled	Not registered	Don't know	Not stated	Total
Full time employee	Satisfied	58.2	60.3	63.0	61.3	60.1
	Neither	26.1	26.7	21.7	24.8	26.7
	Dissatisfied	15.7	12.9	15.2	13.9	13.2
Part time employee	Satisfied	62.9	66.6	90.0	62.5	66.2
	Neither	23.9	23.1	10.0	21.8	23.1
	Dissatisfied	13.2	10.3	–	15.8	10.7
Self employed	Satisfied	59.2	59.8	66.7	60.4	59.7
	Neither	24.6	26.5	33.3	27.8	26.3
	Dissatisfied	16.2	13.7	–	11.9	14.0
Government scheme	Satisfied	61.9	61.6	–	65.0	61.7
	Neither	20.2	25.9	–	20.0	24.0
	Dissatisfied	17.9	12.5	–	15.0	24.0
Full time education	Satisfied	55.1	60.7	50.0	60.4	60.3
	Neither	26.9	27.7	–	8.3	27.5
	Dissatisfied	18.0	11.6	50.0	31.3	12.2
Unemployed	Satisfied	64.0	63.4	75.0	66.7	63.6
	Neither	20.6	22.9	–	18.5	22.2
	Dissatisfied	15.3	13.8	25.0	14.8	14.2
Permanently sick/disabled	Satisfied	64.2	66.5	100 (6)	68.9	64.4
	Neither	20.0	21.3	–	15.8	20.1
	Dissatisfied	15.7	12.2	–	15.3	15.5
Retired	Satisfied	70.4	72.8	69.8	70.8	71.8
	Neither	19.1	18.3	22.1	18.4	18.7
	Dissatisfied	10.5	8.9	8.1	10.8	9.6
Working in the home	Satisfied	69.8	69.4	47.6	70.7	69.5
	Neither	19.4	20.9	28.6	18.0	20.5
	Dissatisfied	10.8	9.7	23.8	11.2	10.0
Doing something else	Satisfied	66.7	65.2	80.0	63.3	65.4
	Neither	20.2	22.7	20.0	22.2	21.9
	Dissatisfied	13.1	12.2	–	14.5	12.7
Not stated	Satisfied	70.1	70.5	60.1	64.9	67.6
	Neither	16.7	18.7	21.0	22.4	22.4
	Dissatisfied	13.1	10.8	19.0	12.8	12.7

**OFFICE OF THE
DEPUTY PRIME MINISTER**

Also Available

Work-Life Balance – a survey of local authorities
This report presents information gathered through a survey of local authorities on work-life balance/flexible arrangements and facilities that affect both employees and the provision of public services. The findings reveal that local authorities, as employers, are leading the agenda in terms of more flexible working practices. The provision of flexible services and facilities is more limited but the benefits offered by new technologies, especially in terms of information provision, are being embraced by most authorities.

Youth Participation in Local Government
This report presents the findings of a qualitative study to investigate the reasons why young people are not participating in local government and consider what might be done to alter this. It demonstrates in considerable depth the different ways in which young people view and participate in local politics, and the factors that shape and influence their individual perspectives. It provides useful insights and solutions that can help inform the invigoration of democratic processes.

Impact of Releasing People for Council Duties
This report investigates the impact on councillors and their employers of the present arrangements for releasing people for council duties. It presents the key findings of two research surveys, one with councillors and the other with their employers, and discusses issues arising from these.

ORDER FORM

Ref/ISBN	Title	Price	Quantity
LG/1 85112 474 8	Work-Life Balance – a survey of local authorities	£10	. . . . . .
LG/1 85112 582 5	Youth Participation in Local Government	£14	. . . . . .
LG/1 85112 088 2	Impact of Releasing People for Council Duties	£30	. . . . . .
		TOTAL	. . . . . .

Send this information with a cheque or postal order made out to **Office of the Deputy Prime Minister** to:

The Office of the Deputy Prime Minister, Publications Sales Centre
PO Box 236, Wetherby, LS23 7NB
Or order using a credit card on Tel: 0870 1226 236
Fax: 0870 1226 237
Textphone: 0870 1207 405
Email: odpm@twoten.press.net